Adam's
Long Shadow

BY JOSEPH STOLL

"Now all these things happened unto them for
ensamples: and they are written for our admonition,
upon whom the ends of the world are come. Wherefore let
him that thinketh he standeth take heed lest he fall."
—1 Corinthians 10:11, 12

Vision Publishers
HARRISONBURG, VA

Adam's Long Shadow
ISBN: 1-932676-09-0
©Joseph Stoll 2008
©Vision Publishers 2008

Scripture quotations are taken from the **King James Version** of
the Holy Scriptures, except as noted. The author took liberty to
paraphrase chosen passages in his contemporary English.

Cover and Text Design: Lonnie D. Yoder
Editors: Timothy Kennedy, John D. Risser and others
Digital Text Entry: Elizabeth B. Burkholder

For additional copies or comments write to:
Vision Publishers
P.O. Box 190
Harrisonburg, VA 22803
Fax: 540/437-1969
Phone: 877/488-0901
E-mail: orders@vision-publishers.com
www.vision-publishers.com
(see order form in back)

Contents

Preface

We learn from our mistakes. Such learning is a part of life. But we also learn from the mistakes of others. We even learn from the mistakes of people who lived long before our time. We take warning from those who fell. Because someone else stumbled, we watch our own steps more closely.

Our Old Order Amish church services follow a regular schedule. Twice each year, during our *Ordnung Gemeinde* services, the sermons consist almost entirely of narrative accounts from the first five books of the Bible. These special *Ordnung Gemeinde* services are a preparation for Communion, which follows two weeks later.

Amish church services usually last three hours, but these special services draw out much longer. Time passes swiftly, however, if the Bible stories are told in an interesting way. I have fond boyhood memories of sitting beside my father on the hard wooden bench, my bare feet dangling, listening raptly to the stories of Cain and Abel, Noah, Abraham and Isaac, Jacob and Esau, Joseph, and Moses and Joshua.

Eventually, it fell to my lot to study those Bible accounts much more thoroughly. For a new generation of children were now seated beside their parents, and they looked to me to preach the age-old stories and draw moral lessons from the lives of Bible patriarchs.

We can learn much from their lives. Some of them made wise choices. Some of them did not. At times, it seems, we learn best from negative examples. In this book we admittedly focus on those. Yet, the object goes far beyond storytelling; our quest is a serious one. We seek moral direction for our own lives. We pray that God will preserve us from sinning as others have sinned. Although we present many lessons from a negative perspective, we trust our readers will apply them to their own lives in a manner that is overwhelmingly positive.

- Joseph Stoll

Introduction

Down through the annals of time there have been many noble men. As we study these accounts, a dark side often is discovered that was not included in the biographies of these great men. The dark side of people's lives is also found on the pages of the biblical record. What good comes from writing about this?

As I read *Adam's Long Shadow*, I discovered some of the reasons for this record. Adam's sin is still much in evidence today. History is repeated again and again. We not only see it all about us, but we continue to experience the same temptations that these Old Testament saints and non-saints succumbed to. Will it never end? Prominent national leaders and church leaders fail. There are unfaithful spouses, broken marriages, and parental delinquency that produce dysfunctional families. There is also drunkenness, drug abuse, murder, rape, pornography, immodest dress, filthy language, and much more. *Adam's Long Shadow* reminds us that people have not changed.

We can learn much from the noble and the ignoble. But do we need to experience all of the missteps in order to learn what God wants us to learn? The Scripture says that these things were written for our learning. The record of men who sinned has been given so that we do not commit the same sins.

Joseph Stoll very ably lifts up the remedy for the long shadow that Adam's sin left with each one of us. That remedy is provided in the second Adam, Jesus Christ. It is found in accepting the atoning sacrifice that Jesus provided for our sins in shedding His blood on the cross.

I highly recommend this book for the warnings it gives and for the hope that it presents.

- H. Eldwin Campbell, *Publisher*

CHAPTER ONE

The Sin of Adam and Eve

The six days of creation were just ended. The earth, the skies, the plants and animals of every description were all newly made by the almighty hand of God. The Creator had crowned His work by forming the man Adam from the dust of the earth and making the woman from the man's rib to be a helper suitable for him. He placed both of them in the beautiful paradise of Eden—the purest, sweetest home man has ever known on earth.*

Life in Eden was bliss. No pain, no sorrow, no hunger, no tears. There were no guilty consciences to mar perfect communion with God. Adam and Eve basked in the sunshine of God's love and favor.

But sadly, this bliss did not last forever. A shadow fell across the garden as the tempter entered. He cast a jealous eye upon the man and the woman and began to plot their downfall. Subtle and cunning, he approached our first parents in the form of a serpent. He was Satan, once an angel but now cast out of heaven, the archenemy of God. He plotted to ruin God's paradise, to spoil the perfectness of creation.

One of the greatest dramas of all time unfolded. Its consequences were so far reaching that only the greater drama

---

*The story of Adam and Eve is found in Genesis 2:7—5:5.

at Golgotha surpasses its power. For there in the Garden of Eden, Satan dared to strike at God's sovereignty. He dared to strike at God's authority in the new world that God had made. Satan wanted no less than to rule in the hearts and souls of the humans God had created.

Adam and Eve were surrounded by God's goodness. Daily they were aware of His blessings, for in the garden grew "every tree that is pleasant to the sight, and good for food." They could eat of the fruit of all of these trees, except one. God had explained it clearly to Adam.

> Of every tree of the garden thou mayest freely eat: but of the tree of the knowledge of good and evil, thou shalt not eat of it: for in the day that thou eatest thereof thou shalt surely die (Genesis 2:16, 17).

Under circumstances such as these, the man and woman had every reason to be faithful to God. Satan could hardly hope to lure them away from such overwhelming providence.

The Temptation

When Satan approached the woman in Eden, he lacked experience. This was a new pursuit for him. Never before had he been given the opportunity to tempt a human to sin. Though this was his first attempt, Satan could hardly have planned his strategy better. His tactics proved so successful, that he has not needed to change them down through the years. Let us note carefully how he tempted our first parents.

1. *He came disguised as a serpent.* Satan came to Eve under false pretenses. He did not announce that he was the devil, the enemy of God. Had he done so, Eve no doubt would have fled. Instead, he came in the form of a snake, to Eve a harm-

less animal of the field. And thus the tempter still comes to us today, pretending to be what he is not.

2. *He came to Eve, instead of to Adam.* She was the weaker vessel, and through her he hoped to reach Adam, as, indeed, he succeeded to do. Satan still finds this trick useful, tempting us through our friends and companions.

3. *He came to Eve when she was near the forbidden tree,* or so it seems. It would have been better if she had been in a far corner of the garden. Those who hope to keep from sinning should keep themselves at a safe distance.

4. *Satan tempted Eve by asking a question.* "Yea, hath God said, Ye shall not eat of every tree of the garden?" Oh, how subtle was this question! Thus he accomplished two things. First, he planted a doubt in the woman's mind. "Yea, hath God said? Do you think it is really true? Did God actually mean what He said?" Second, by his question he lured Eve into talking with him. She would have done better had she turned her back on the serpent and gone home to her husband, without speaking a word.

5. *Satan lied to Eve.* He is the father of lies[1] and could not long hide his true colors. God had said, "Thou shalt surely die," but Satan contradicted those words saying, "Ye shall not surely die." The devil does not hesitate to lie.

With a mixture of deceit and false promises, Satan flattered Eve: "God doth know that in the day ye eat thereof, your eyes shall be opened, and ye shall be as gods, knowing good and evil." He promised them rewards and betterment, if they would but eat of the forbidden fruit.

The Sin

Eve should have known better. The tempter's words were simply not true, could not be true. God had never mistreated them. There was nothing in Eve's past to cause her to doubt God's love and concern.

But the temptation had taken root in Eve's mind, and she could no longer think clearly. Her eyes were drawn to the forbidden fruit, now so enticing and so desirable. No matter that the trees roundabout were hanging heavy with delicious fruit. All that mattered to Eve was the tree of the knowledge of good and evil, its fruit the more attractive because it was not lawful.

Looking on the fruit was in itself a dangerous step toward sin. Eve had no doubt glanced at the fruit before, but now she looked at it longingly. She "saw that the tree was good for food, and that it was pleasant to the eyes, and a tree to be desired to make one wise."

After looking, Eve took. The Bible says simply, "She took of the fruit thereof." She took it of her own free will, of her own choice. The devil did not break off the fruit and place it in her mouth. Eve took it herself.

Even so, the fatal act may not have yet been committed. The woman had been unwise to look on the fruit. She had made a mistake to pluck it off the tree. But there was still hope, because she had not eaten of it. Could she stop now? We learn from the Book of James that it was not likely that she would. "When lust hath conceived, it bringeth forth sin; and sin, when it is finished, bringeth forth death."[2] Then Eve ate the forbidden fruit. The deed was done. Satan must have smiled to himself as he watched. He had reason to smile even more as the next act unfolded. For now, after the sin was committed, Eve gave the fruit to her husband. Eve herself had become a temptress. No sooner had she become a sinner, than she tempted her husband to sin as well. Adam followed her example and ate of it also.

The transgression was complete. Sin forced open the door to Eden and came marching in. The purity of the garden was spoiled, its perfection forever marred. Gone was the guiltlessness, the peace, the plenty. Now there was agonizing fear, crushing shame, a burden of remorse. In their bewildered state, Adam and Eve hid from the presence of God.

The man and the woman had been put to the test, and they had failed. They had fallen.

The Punishment

Sin always has its penalty. God had warned Adam, "In the day that thou eatest thereof thou shalt surely die." The human mind hardly comprehends the far-reaching extent of those words, the huge price that sin was to exact from mankind.

The sin of Adam and Eve brought with it, first of all, death. Not only did sin rupture their spiritual relationship with God, it brought natural death to mankind. From the moment of his fall, Adam was a dying man. He was no more clothed with immortality, but his body would grow old and feeble until at last it would return to the dust from which it had been taken.

Sin brought death. But it brought more. God pronounced a curse and a judgment upon the three parties involved in the transgression—the serpent, the woman, and the man.

God's sentence upon the serpent was severe.

> Because thou hast done this, thou art cursed above all cattle, and above every beast of the field: upon thy belly shalt thou go, and dust shalt thou eat all the days of thy life: And I will put enmity between thee and the woman, and between thy seed and her seed: it shall bruise thy head, and thou shalt bruise his heel (Genesis 3:14, 15).

Satan had won a victory, but it was not a final one. With these words, God promised the Redeemer, who in the fullness of time would make atonement for sin. Jesus, "the seed of the woman," would crush the head of Satan and gain victory over death. The Promised One would restore eternal life to man.

Adam and Eve could only look forward to that great redemption. The sin and suffering they had introduced to the human race must bear its harvest.

For Eve God foretold much suffering because of her sin.

> I will greatly multiply thy sorrow and thy conception; in sorrow thou shalt bring forth children: and thy desire shall be to thy husband, and he shall rule over thee (Genesis 3:16).

And to Adam, God's words were likewise stern:

> Cursed is the ground for thy sake; in sorrow shalt thou eat of it all the days of thy life; thorns also and thistles shall it bring forth to thee; and thou shalt eat the herb of the field; in the sweat of thy face shalt thou eat bread, till thou return unto the ground; for out of it wast thou taken: for dust thou art, and unto dust shalt thou return (Genesis 3:17-19).

Sorrow and curses, thorns and thistles, sweat and toil and, at last, the body returning to the earth from which it was taken. What a contrast to the peaceful bliss before the fall! Adam and Eve paid heavily for their disobedience. They may have realized in full what sin had cost them only after they lost their two oldest sons, when Cain struck Abel dead in the field. The serpent had not mentioned anything like this!

They were no longer in Eden. God drove them out of the beautiful garden and placed cherubim and a shining sword that turned every way to guard the entrance.

No other sin brought such woeful results as did the sin of Adam and Eve in the garden of Eden. Because of their transgression, a sinful nature became the heritage of every human born into the world.

The sin of Adam and Eve lives on, though six thousand years have passed. Their experience is hauntingly similar to the temptations and sins we know today. Their offense—disobedience—still lies at the heart of all evil.

But praise be to God that He sent His only Son to earth to undo the havoc caused by Adam's sin. The tragedy of Eden has been swallowed up by the victory won in another garden, Gethsemane. By His obedience, Jesus has provided an escape from the condemnation and judgment that resulted from Adam's sin.

The Apostle Paul summed up Jesus' triumph in his letter to the Romans:

> Wherefore, as by one man sin entered into the world, and death by sin; and so death passed upon all men, for that all have sinned. . . . Therefore, as by the offense of one, judgment came upon all men to condemnation, even so by the righteousness of one the free gift came upon all men unto justification of life. For as by one man's disobedience many were made sinners, so by the obedience of one shall many be made righteous (Romans 5:12, 18, 19).

---

1. John 8:44.
2. James 1:15.

CHAPTER TWO

The Sins of Noah's Generation

Is there a sadder story in the Bible than the story of Adam and Eve eating the forbidden fruit? Hardly. Yet there is a story almost as sad: the story of the Flood.

Sin spread, until the whole earth was filled with iniquity.* At last, the world became so evil that God was sorry He had created man. So God caused a great flood to come upon the earth, and all the people drowned except the eight righteous souls in Noah's ark.

Why should God think it necessary to wipe from the face of the earth all but a remnant of what He had created? What kind of sin doomed the first world to destruction?

Men in those days lived to a great age. Adam did not die until he was 930 years old. By that time, at least nine generations of his descendants were living on the earth. In the line of Seth there were many righteous men faithfully serving God. There was godly Enoch, the seventh from Adam, who was already prophesying the coming of the Lord to execute judgment upon the ungodly.[1] This same Enoch walked with God,[2] and only a few years after the death of Adam, he was taken from the earth to be with God.

---

*The story of Noah's generation is found in Genesis 5:29—9:29.

Meanwhile, the descendants of Cain had multiplied and increased greatly. They were a worldly-minded and wicked people. Clever and intelligent, they were known for their inventions and their craftsmanship. They built great cities.[3]

Noah was born to the godly house of Lamech.[4] He was the tenth generation from Adam, and his birth occurred in the year 1056 after the Creation. His father, Lamech, had been born while Adam was still alive. As Noah grew up, he likely heard his father relate the Creation account and the story of the fall of man.

But as the years passed, the world changed. One by one, the older men of faith died. Cain's descendants grew bolder and crowded close together in their wickedness. The younger men of the godly families were influenced by the worldliness about them. Sin crept in, little by little, becoming the accepted thing. As Noah looked about him, he must have been dismayed by the apostasy taking place. He must have been perplexed and discouraged as his own relatives forsook the true worship of God to live in sin.

The Bible speaks strongly about the sins of Noah's generation—the sins that brought the flood waters swirling over the earth. These sins are alarmingly familiar today. Christ foretold this very thing when He said, "As it was in the days of Noah, so shall it be also in the days of the Son of man."[5]

Before the Flood, people were guilty of four major types of wickedness. These same sins will be prevalent in the last days, just before Jesus comes the second time.

Mixed Marriages

The opening verses of Genesis 6 tell us what brought the downfall and spiritual ruin of God's people.

And it came to pass, when men began to multiply on the face of the earth, and daughters were born unto them, that the sons of God saw the daughters of men that they were fair; and they took them wives of all which they chose (Genesis 6:1, 2).

These mixed marriages could have but one result—the breakdown of the home. In a few generations the worship of God was completely lost.

Even in those long-ago days, there had to be separation between the just and the unjust, the righteous and the wicked. If this separation was maintained, the faith of God's people could be preserved. It could be passed on to succeeding generations. However, when the righteous began to socialize with and to marry the wicked, the barriers were broken down and the old standards crumbled.

Sin flourished as never before. The offspring of mixed marriages became mighty men of renown. They were known for their daring, their worldly wisdom, their business skills, or their great learning. The inherited virtues and values of many generations of godly men and women were turned into lasciviousness, cunning, and violence.

It was not long before God pronounced the coming terrible judgment.

God saw that the wickedness of man was great in the earth, and that every imagination of the thoughts of his heart was only evil continually. And it repented the Lord that he had made man on the earth, and it grieved him at his heart (Genesis 6:5, 6).

How disappointed, indeed, must God have been! As He looked down upon the descendants of Adam, now numerous upon the face of the earth, their sin grieved Him greatly. Evil and disobedience were so widespread, so universal, that it broke His heart.

The Earth Was Corrupt

That people in Noah's day were very corrupt is twice mentioned in as many verses.

> The earth also was corrupt before God . . . and God looked upon the earth, and behold, it was corrupt: for all flesh had corrupted his way upon the earth (Genesis 6:11, 12).

The family of Cain had always been corrupt, but now godly families blended with them and were also corrupted.

This corruption was probably manifest in many ways. The members of what had been godly families could no longer be trusted. As their faith in God was lost, so was their virtue. They were no longer upright or honest, no longer pure-thinking, respectful, and law-abiding citizens.

In place of virtues, evil habits crept in—swearing, joking about sacred matters, eating and drinking to excess. Men's thoughts and their deeds became immoral. The world was full of rank liars and scoundrels, perverted and depraved men who plotted wickedness night and day. And they boasted proudly of their sinful plans. The Bible says that every imagination of the thoughts of their hearts was only evil continually.

They were a pleasure-loving people, serving the flesh with abandon. Jesus tells us that they were "eating and drinking, marrying and giving in marriage, until the day that Noah entered into the ark."[6] The people of Noah's time ate and drank and married in a carnal way, finding their utmost pleasure in these things. They heaped up treasures on earth:

lands and houses, bank accounts and full tables, wedding feasts and revelry.

Noah in his lifetime saw a great degeneration in morals. God's law of marriage was often violated. Broken homes, illegitimate children, deserted wives—all these were, without doubt, rampant in the great corruption of Noah's day.

In the midst of this people wandered Noah, a lonely man, nearly overwhelmed by the corruption around him, yet steadfastly preaching righteousness.

The Earth Filled With Violence

The earth was not only corrupt, it was full of violence, as Genesis mentions twice.

Godly people are gentle by nature, kind and peace-loving. The wicked are the opposite. As the world became more corrupt, violence flared. Murder, beatings, robbery, and bloodshed multiplied. Now the first murderer, Cain, had many followers. As the number of men grew, blood flowed more freely. The wicked plotted dark crimes by day and carried them out by night. If violence was common, tribal wars and fightings were certain to have occurred.

Were the righteous persecuted in those days? It is quite possible. We read of only one martyr who died for his faith before the flood (Abel), but there may have been more. Perhaps the most alarming of all was the violence that men did to their consciences, trampling underfoot their faith in God.

They Did Not Repent

Another great sin of Noah's generation was their rejection of Noah's preaching. God did not destroy the people without first giving them a chance to repent. As 1 Peter 3:20 explains, God was long-suffering. He waited while Noah prepared the ark. If Noah's generation had repented as did the people of Nineveh, God would surely have spared them.

Jesus tells us that the people continued in their sins right up to the day of the Flood. They paid absolutely no attention to the prophet in their midst, nor to the great ark of gopher wood. Certainly, they had cause to marvel as the animals came from all directions and filed into the ark. However, in Matthew 24, we read that they kept right on in their sins.

> For as in the days that were before the flood, they were eating and drinking, marrying and giving in marriage, until the day that Noah entered into the ark, And knew not until the flood came, and took them all away; so shall also the coming of the Son of man be (Matthew 24:38, 39).

Thus the people hardened their hearts and rejected Noah's warning cry. This was their final transgression—refusing God's call to repentance. They had disobeyed God in so many ways, had become a corrupt and a violent people, yet God was long-suffering toward them. It was only after they had rejected the ark of salvation, God's offer of redemption, that He saw fit to destroy them. This final sin brought the flood waters at last.

As It Was in the Days of Noah

Even if Christ had not compared the time before His second coming with the days before the Flood, it would be hard to escape the fact that today's conditions are very similar to those in Noah's day. In the past century, we have seen sweeping changes in the world, such as have not been known since the time of Noah. These changes continue, and we do not know how long God's patience will delay before He once again calls for judgment on the earth. We do know that Christ will then come in a cloud with power and great glory, with a shout and the voice of the archangel and the trumpet of God. Then He will gather His elect from the four winds of heaven.[7]

Was the earth before the Flood more corrupt than it is today? We live in an age of increasing cheating, dishonesty, and immorality. There is bribery in high places. Fraud and shoplifting are commonplace. Ours is a pleasure-loving age, abundant with leisure and flush with cash. The earth is corrupt.

We live in a violent world also. The two greatest wars the earth has ever known were fought in the 20th century. Horrific inventions such as nuclear bombs, fighter planes, and guided missiles have increased war's slaughter. A steady rise in crime and violence causes us to wonder if the world could have been more violent in the days of Noah than it is today!

A mark of Noah's times was marrying and giving in marriage. Does this indicate frequent divorce and remarrying? How might today's divorce rate compare? Are marriages more stable today than they were in the days of Noah? In some areas of the United States, there are as many divorces in a year as there are marriages.

The worldly person seeks pleasure and ease and security. He gives himself gladly to the fads and fashions of the day. He makes the movie star and the pop singer his heroes. He fills his home with gadgets—the idols of the modern world. The TV blinks and blares in his living room; the automobile purrs in his garage. He leans back in his easy chair and sips cold beer. He puffs on a cigarette and eats and drinks himself to an early, and overweight, death.

This is all very disturbing. But then, we have been describing the world—the sinners who make no pretense of godliness.

One can hardly expect better of them.

We have not yet mentioned the most alarming situation of the day, which is to see these same desires, these same attitudes in the church. This is truly cause for concern. For we remember what happened in Noah's day when the sons of God began to identify with the daughters of men.

God calls His people, the church, to live lives that will set them apart from a wicked world. Values and expressions should be different. It is sad when those who call themselves Christians cannot be distinguished from non-Christians. And yet, is it not so in our day?[8]

Worldliness increasingly shows up in churches. The proud spirit, worldly dress, worldly desires. What is happening? Too many young people do not care for the true faith. They lack convictions against the evils of our day. Light-minded, silly joking is common on the lips of even older people. Traveling for pleasure abounds, as do hunting and fishing trips. People feast and overeat. Weddings are luxurious, courtships immoral. Discipline is slack in homes, schools, and alas, in churches.

Are we not living in a day of apostasy, just as Noah did? Our greatest marriage problem is within the church—the spiritual adultery of the Bride of Jesus Christ.

Noah's neighbors would feel at home in our world. But Noah would be distressed.

The Ark of the New Testament

The final sin of Noah's generation was their refusal to heed Noah's warning, to repent and enter into the ark before the flood waters fell. Only eight souls were lifted by the ark above the raging waters—Noah, his wife, his three sons, and their wives. What a pitifully small number, compared to the hosts that drowned!

Those living today have a similar opportunity to repent. And once more an ark has been prepared, an escape provided: the ark of the New Testament of Jesus Christ. Through His blood and sacrifice on the cross, salvation is possible—an eternal salvation much superior to Noah's ark.

But there are conditions to be met, just as there were conditions for Noah. These conditions are repentance, new birth, and living the new life in Christ faithfully until death. Only Noah and his family were qualified to enter the ark, and only those meeting these conditions are qualified to enter the ark of the New Testament.

The Bible does not say how many righteous will be alive when Christ comes again, but we are told there will be "a falling away first,"[9] before the end. Jesus Himself said few would be saved, compared to the multitudes who are lost.

The majority of people will continue in their sins right up to the last hour, paying no heed to God and His Word. They will be like the people of Noah's day, who were caught by the Flood while they were still eating and drinking, marrying and giving in marriage.

Only a faithful few will be ready and waiting, as Christ advised them.

> Watch therefore: for ye know not what hour your Lord doth come. Therefore be ye also ready: for in such an hour as ye think not the Son of man cometh (Matthew 24:42, 44).

What can we learn from the life of Noah? Very much. His life encourages us to stand true as he did, not letting ourselves be corrupted by the worldliness around us, not weakening just because we are in the minority.

What a contrast was Noah's life to the sin and wickedness round about him! How he must have pled with his neighbors! How he must have suffered when they laughed at him!

Yet Noah did not falter. He did not waver. He knew he was right. He felt God's approval like a comforting balm upon his troubled soul.

> Noah found grace in the eyes of the Lord.... Noah was a just man, and perfect in his generations. And Noah walked with God. . . . Thus did Noah, according to all that God commanded him, so did he (Genesis 6:8, 9, 22).

---

1. See Jude 14.
2. Genesis 5:21-24; Hebrews 11:3.
3. Genesis 4:16-22.
4. Genesis 5:28, 29.
5. Matthew 24:36-39; Luke 17:26, 27.
6. Matthew 24:37-39.
7. Matthew 24:31; Mark 13:27.
8. 2 Corinthians 6:14-18; 1 Peter 2:9, 10.
9. 2 Thessalonians 2:2, 3.

CHAPTER THREE

Lot and the Sins of Sodom

It was a strange call that came to Abraham: "Get thee out of thy country, and from thy kindred, and from thy father's house, unto a land that I will show thee." God had singled out Abraham and had given him the promise, "In thee shall all families of the earth be blessed."

Abraham left his home in obedience to God's call, but he did not go alone. His nephew, the son of his deceased brother, decided to go with him. This nephew's name was Lot.

The story of Lot's life begins well, but it ends sadly.* He went out with Abraham, obedient to the heavenly call. He did not know where God might be leading his uncle, but Lot went along. Years later we find this same Lot a homeless outcast on the mountain, a broken old man who had lost his wife, the drunken victim of his own daughters' scheming. Lot had lost great riches. He had lost his position of honor among men. And he had all but lost his family.

At some point, Lot had made a mistake. What could it have been?

Lot Chooses

As long as Lot had pitched his tent alongside his uncle's, he had shared in Abraham's blessings. But the time came when

---

*The story of Lot is found in Genesis 11:27–12:5; 13:1-13; 18:1–19:38; 2 Peter 2:1-9.

a problem developed between Abraham and his nephew. Their flocks and herds had grown so large, there was not enough grass for them all.

God had promised the land to Abraham and his descendants. So, Lot was not included in the promise. But Abraham was big-hearted and unselfish, saying to his nephew, "If thou wilt take the left hand, then I will go to the right; or if thou depart to the right hand, then I will go to the left."

The choice lay before Lot, who should have replied, "Oh, no, Uncle Abraham. It is not right for me to choose first. God has given you this land, and it is yours. It is not mine. But if you wish to set aside a few pastures for my livestock, I will be grateful. You decide."

Instead, Lot rather greedily took advantage of his uncle's offer. He cast his eyes over the plains of Jordan, green and well-watered and dotted with cities. Grass and water and markets. What more could a stockman ask for?

Lot was at heart a God-fearing man. The New Testament describes him as a righteous man. So it may well be that Lot was troubled by his choice. The cities of the plain had a bad reputation. The people of Sodom and the neighboring towns were exceedingly wicked.

Toward Sodom

Abraham and Lot parted. For some time Abraham did not move from his mountain camp east of Bethel. But Lot pulled up his tent stakes, rounded up his flocks and herds, and headed down the hill toward the Jordan Valley.

There lay Sodom below him, far in the distance. I doubt that Lot was planning to live in the evil city. The very thought may have shocked him.

The Bible says simply, "He pitched his tent toward Sodom." Surely, it was Lot's greatest mistake. For in the end, Lot found himself at home inside the city walls. We do not know just how it came about. He hardly expected to become a citizen of Sodom when he first left his Uncle Abraham and came down the mountain to pitch his tent in the plain.

How familiar the story sounds even today. Many a man has made a choice like Lot's. Many a person has faced the decision to turn to the left or to the right. As the grassy, well-watered plains drew Lot, so the modern world with its conveniences and riches and ease seem desirable to many. It is a dangerous thing to pitch one's tent toward Sodom, unless one has no objection to eventually living there.

Life in Sodom

The time came when Lot and his family were actual residents of Sodom, the thriving but wicked city of the plains. It is hard to imagine a godly man bringing his family into such an environment; yet Lot did so. Perhaps his wife and his children were the ones who wished to live in Sodom, and Lot was too weak to oppose them.

But was Sodom really such a bad place to live? Indeed it was. The Bible says the people of Sodom were extremely wicked, "sinners before the Lord exceedingly." They were immoral, but they were also sinful in other, more common ways. The prophet Ezekiel tells us their iniquity was threefold. The first sin was *pride*—a haughtiness and rebellion against God. The second was *fullness of bread*—gluttony and feasting. The third was *abundance of idleness*—a spirit of leisure.[1]

The most shocking of Sodom's sins was certainly its immorality. When two angels came to Sodom as Lot's guests, the men of Sodom burned with perverted lust and tried to break down Lot's door to get at the visitors. When the angels struck them blind, they still would not forget their lust, but "wearied themselves to find the door."

Why did Lot make his home in such a city? Why did he not flee with his family to a place more suited to godly living? We know that Lot was troubled and saddened. In 2 Peter 2:8 we read, "For that righteous man dwelling among them, in seeing and hearing, vexed his righteous soul from day to day with their unlawful deeds."

Still, Lot and his family were reluctant to leave Sodom the morning it was to be destroyed. The angels urged them to arise and get out lest they be consumed with the city. And yet, Lot lingered.

It was hard for Lot to leave. Why, we do not know. It may have been his fine home, his riches, or a position of honor in the city. It may have been his sons-in-law, who had laughed at him when he warned them to leave. Lot was too well at home in Sodom. The messengers of God took Lot by the hand and pulled him from the city.

It took more than human determination for Lot to get out of the city, and even after he was safely outside, he lost his wife, for she looked back at what they had left and became a pillar of salt. How hard it is to break free from a Sodom!

Lot's troubles began the day he selfishly chose the grassy plains for his cattle. From that moment on, Lot suffered: a weak man growing weaker. What a contrast to his earlier "going-out" with Abraham!

It is a sad story of a godly man who yielded to worldly pressures, barely escaping with his soul. The mistakes he made are a warning to us all.

---

1. Ezekiel 16:49, 50.

CHAPTER FOUR

The Sin of Korah, the Rebel

Few sins are more dangerous, or more damaging, than rebellion. Rebellion may begin slowly, but it grows into a monster raging out of control.

Consider Korah's story.* To bring the children of Israel out of Egypt and through the wilderness to Canaan, God chose a strong but humble leader—Moses. God chose Aaron to assist Moses by serving as high priest. These two brothers were divinely appointed for a difficult task. Moses and Aaron would never have succeeded if God had not been the Supreme Leader, for the Israelites were a murmuring, stiff-necked nation. The day came when some of them rose up to challenge Moses and Aaron, rebelling against their authority.

Korah was the rebellious ringleader. He was already a man of influence in the tribe of Levi, but he had greater ambitions. It was too much for Korah to humble himself beneath Moses and Aaron. He could not see why Aaron's family alone should be priests. Was Aaron a wiser or more talented man than Korah? Were Aaron's sons more holy than the sons of other Levites?

Korah did not keep his questions to himself. He sought out sympathetic listeners. As Korah whispered to others how

---

*The story of Korah is found in Numbers 16.

unfair it was, the seeds of rebellion began to grow and to spread in Israel.

Korah was especially attracted to two men of the tribe of Reuben—Dathan and Abiram. These two men were jealous of Moses, while Korah coveted Aaron's position. Perhaps Dathan and Abiram thought Israel's leader should be a Reubenite. Was not Reuben the eldest of Jacob's sons?

We shall see what became of Korah and his friends. From their fate we can learn how serious it is to rebel.

Korah's Challenge

When Korah and his friends thought the moment was ripe, they gathered their forces and appeared before Moses and Aaron. They did not come for a friendly discussion, or to talk politics. They came on business, and they were in earnest.

It was a menacing group that confronted Moses and Aaron. Korah had laid his plot well. With him, besides Dathan and Abiram, were two hundred and fifty men, not common laborers of the field, but princes of the assembly, men who were widely known and respected. A petition from such a group could not be taken lightly.

From a human standpoint, it looked as though Moses and Aaron would have to resign. Their term of leadership had expired.

Korah spoke confidently to Moses and Aaron.

> You take too much upon you, seeing all the congregation are holy, every one of them, and the LORD is among them: wherefore then lift ye up yourselves above the congregation of the LORD? (Numbers 16:3).

Moses was shocked and dismayed. He fell upon his face and prayed. He needed wisdom from God to deal with this rebellion. When he rose up, he addressed the crowd.

> Tomorrow the LORD will show who are his, and who is holy; . . . even him whom he hath chosen will he cause to come near unto him. This do; Take you censers, Korah, and all his company; And put fire therein, and put incense in them before the LORD tomorrow: and it shall be that the man whom the LORD doth choose, he shall be holy (Numbers 16:5-7).

It was a good answer, but Moses was not yet finished. "You take too much upon you, you sons of Levi," he rebuked them. "Does it seem like a small thing that God has chosen you to do the service of the tabernacle? Do you seek the priesthood also? You are gathered against the Lord, and what is Aaron that you murmur against him?"

In truth, Korah was not rebelling against Moses and Aaron, but against God, who had chosen them for the work.

But Dathan and Abiram of the tribe of Reuben were not present when Moses answered Korah, so Moses sent for them to come to him.

They sent back a defiant reply, "We will not come up. Is it a small thing that you brought us up out of a land of milk and honey to kill us in the wilderness, without making yourself altogether a prince over us?"

Such disrespect! And how twisted and untrue were the charges! Egypt had been a land of hardship and bondage, and they had gladly left it. Whose fault was it that they were still in the wilderness? Certainly it was not Moses' fault. Nor did

Moses desire to rule over them. God had chosen him for the task; he had not chosen himself.

They had forgotten, too, how often Moses had prayed for them and saved them from the just wrath of God. They had forgotten how humbly and meekly he had led them, and how God's power had been made manifest again and again by the hand of Moses. They had forgotten the miraculous crossing of the Red Sea. They had forgotten the water flowing from the rock, the manna and the quail, the thunder of Mt. Sinai, and many other wonders of the wilderness journey.

No, Dathan and Abiram were unable to see matters in their true light. They were deceived, blinded to the truth because of their rebellion.

Once more Moses turned to Korah and commanded him and all his followers to appear with their censers before the Lord the following day. God would then judge between them.

Judgment Is Passed

The next morning, a large crowd gathered before the tabernacle, Korah at their head. Moses and Aaron were there too. This day, God would show how He deals with rebellion.

Perhaps some of the people were only curious and had come to watch the scene. But it appears that most of them were in sympathy with Korah, for God suddenly threatened to destroy them all. Moses and Aaron fell upon their faces, praying, "Shall one man sin, and will You be angry with the whole congregation?"

At God's urging, Moses cried out to the people, "Depart, I pray you, from the tents of these wicked men, and touch nothing of theirs, lest you be consumed in all their sins."

Quickly the people scattered, but Dathan and Abiram remained, boldly standing in the door of their tents. And Moses said,

> Hereby you shall know that the Lord hath sent me to do all these works; for I have not done them of mine own mind. If these men die the common death of all men, or if they be visited after the visitation of all men; then the Lord hath not sent me. But if the LORD make a new thing, and the earth open her mouth and swallow them up, . . . then you shall understand that these men have provoked the LORD (Numbers 16:28, 30, free translation).

Moses had barely finished speaking when the earth opened up and the rebel leaders tumbled in, with all that belonged to them. The Israelites ran to get away, afraid that the earth would break open under them too. Then fire fell and burned up the two hundred and fifty men who had offered incense.

Judgment had been swift and unmistakable. The children of Israel could know that God had chosen Moses and Aaron, and that to rebel against them was to rebel against the Lord. The Israelites had learned a lesson they would not soon forget. Surely the spirit of rebellion among them had been completely destroyed.

But, no, the saddest part of the story is yet to come. Korah's rebellion was like a cancer, penetrating to the very bones of the Israelites. The very next day, a murmur arose among all the congregation against Moses and Aaron, "Ye have killed the people of the Lord."

God had no more patience with such a rebellious nation. He wanted to destroy them all. But once more, Moses and

Aaron fell upon their faces, interceding and praying that God would spare them.

God heard their prayer, though this second day's rebellion cost more lives than the first. This time 14,700 Israelites died of a plague. They might have all died, had not Aaron, the type and forerunner of Jesus Christ, run in among them with his censer to make atonement for the people.

Korah lived in the days of the Old Testament. But rebellion is no less a sin in the sight of God today than it was then. Rebellion still carries with it the price of death—eternal spiritual death. As Aaron the high priest made atonement for the rebellious Israelites, so the only atonement for this sin today is through the shed blood of a greater High Priest, Jesus.

To rebel against divinely-appointed authority on earth is the same as rebelling against God. Governments have authority over their citizens.[1] Parents have authority over their children,[2] husbands over their wives[3] and, finally, ministers over churches.[4] These authority patterns are instituted by God and approved by Him.

There are few virtues more valuable to the Christian than the virtue of humble submission to authority. There are few sins more destructive to the Christian home and church than a lack of respect for authority.

Rebellion sounds like a big, bad word, and it is. But rebellion often starts with small things, things that do not appear so frightening. Rebellion can begin around the family table, when ministers or teachers are "run down" and belittled. It can lie hidden in attitudes that we are not aware are showing. It can come cloaked in a coat of many colors, mixed with truth, sugar-coated with zeal and "praise-the-Lord's"; yet rebellion always boils down to deadly poison—an abomination before God.

A rebellious spirit brings a sure harvest. There may be an attempt to get out from under the despised authority, or to run away from it. Or as did Korah, to overthrow it. In any case, the final and sure outcome of rebellion, if not repented of, is death.

---

1. Romans 13:1-7.
2. Ephesians 6:1-3.
3. Ephesians 5:22, 23.
4. Hebrews 13:17.

CHAPTER FIVE

The Sins of Balaam

The children of Israel were nearing the end of their wilderness wanderings. As they pitched their tents on the plains near Jordan, their presence alarmed Moab and Midian. Balak, the king of Moab, was very much afraid of the Israelites, and he began to look for a way to defeat them.

Balak knew of a prophet who lived in distant Mesopotamia. This prophet, Balaam, was known far and wide. Balak now turned to him for help.*

"Come now, therefore," he sent word to Balaam, "and curse this people that are come out of Egypt, that cover the face of the earth. They are too mighty for me."

Thus begins the story of Balaam. It is the story of an unusual man—a man who professed to seek God's will, yet sinned gravely against God and the children of Israel. Balaam's sins are mentioned three times in the New Testament as a warning to believers. So it should be worthwhile to study his life, to try to understand in what manner Balaam fell.

The Prophet Is Tempted

The messengers from King Balak had brought along gifts for the prophet, to encourage him to come with them. From

---

*The story of Balaam is found in Numbers 22—25; 31:8, 16; Deuteronomy 23:4, 5.

the beginning, Balaam secretly wanted to go, yet outwardly he used restraint. He said to the princes of Moab, "Lodge here tonight, and I will bring you word again, as the Lord shall speak to me."

That night God spoke to Balaam, "Thou shalt not go with them; thou shalt not curse the people: for they are blessed."

God's answer was brief and to the point. If Balaam had been willing to accept it, there would have been no problem. The case would have been closed, and King Balak would have looked elsewhere for help.

But Balaam was disappointed by God's reply. He dismissed Balak's messengers with a few curt words, "Get you into your land: for the Lord refuseth to give me leave to go with you."

From this we observe Balaam's first great sin. He was not willing to accept God's decision. He was not submissive in his heart. He rebelled because his own secret plans and desires had been crossed.

Balaam's attitude was the seedbed of other and greater sins. They were not long in coming to fruit.

The messengers came back to the king, saying merely, "Balaam refuseth to come with us." Naturally, Balak decided the prophet was holding out for more money. He rounded up another delegation, with more men, more honorable ones at that, and sent them off to Balaam again, with this message,

> Let nothing, I pray thee, hinder thee from coming unto me: For I will promote thee unto very great honor, and I will do whatever thou sayest unto me: come therefore, I pray thee, curse me this people (Numbers 22:16, 17).

Balaam's immediate answer to these messengers is not to be despised. He said, "If Balak would give me his house full of silver and gold, I cannot go beyond the word of the Lord my God, to do less or more."

It was a noble statement—had Balaam really believed it and lived up to it. But he did not. At once we find him longing to go to Balak, hoping that God would change His mind, wanting to ask God again. Here, perhaps, Balaam fell into his greatest error. He longed for the riches and honor that Balak had promised him, and this caused him to compromise. He became a man of divided loyalties. A man who wished to serve both God and mammon. He rendered lip service to the God of Israel, but hired himself out to Israel's enemies.

Balaam should have sent the messengers back to Balak with a clear statement that God had said no. That, once again, would have settled the matter. But Balaam said, "Tarry ye also here this night, that I may know what the Lord will say unto me more."

It was a dangerous thing to do. For we learn from this incident, as from other Biblical examples, that God does not always resist the willful person. If Balaam was determined to go, God would not stand in his way. That night He granted the prophet permission to go with the messengers, yet warned him to do only as God commanded him.

Balaam Is Rebuked

We cannot help wondering how Balaam felt as he got up early the next morning to saddle his ass. Was he happy and cheerful that God had changed His mind? Or was he sober and conscience-stricken, feeling guilty about it all? He had failed to submit his will to God's. He had failed to crucify his own selfish desire for earthly wealth and honor. And yet, he must have felt bound by God's strict warning, "The word that I shall say unto thee, that shalt thou do."

No doubt, Balaam started on the long ride to Moab with mixed feelings. On the road that day, God made it known that He was not only displeased with Balaam, He was angry. He sent His angel with a drawn sword to stand in Balaam's way. Balaam's ass saw the angel and three times tried to escape, so that at last Balaam lost his temper and hit the beast with his staff.

God then used the ass to rebuke Balaam. Speaking with a man's voice, the donkey said, "What have I done unto thee that thou hast smitten me these three times?"

Balaam was so angry, he gave no thought to how miraculous it was for an ass to speak, but bitterly declared, "I wish I had a sword in my hand, then I would kill you."

Suddenly Balaam's eyes were opened, and he saw the angel of the Lord with his sword drawn. The angel rebuked Balaam: "I went out to withstand thee, because thy way is perverse before me."

Balaam was cornered. He was defeated. So he admitted, perhaps sullenly, "I have sinned. . . . Now therefore if it displease thee, I will get me back again."

But God allowed Balaam to continue on to Moab. As he traveled forward, Balaam was still the same man. He had not repented of his greed, nor of his spirit of compromise.

Balaam Meets Balak

King Balak came out to meet the prophet and welcome him to Moab. The very next day the king took Balaam up to a high place from which he could look down upon the tents of Israel.

Three times Balaam offered bullocks and rams on seven altars, and three times God spoke to the prophet. But instead of a curse upon Israel as both Balak and Balaam had hoped for, God's message was each time a blessing upon Israel. The third time, there was even a prophecy of the coming Messiah, "A Star out of Jacob, and a Sceptre shall rise out of Israel. . . ."

King Balak was greatly upset. After the second blessing, he cried out to Balaam, "If you cannot curse them, then do not bless them either!" But Balaam could not help himself. He was under God's control. God had turned Balaam's plottings to His own benefit. Rather than curses upon Israel, the unwilling prophet showered blessings upon them.

Later, Moses said to the Israelites,

> [Moab] hired against thee Balaam the son of Beor . . . to curse thee. Nevertheless the LORD thy God would not hearken unto Balaam; but the LORD thy God turned the curse into a blessing unto thee, because the LORD thy God loved thee (Deuteronomy 23:4, 5).

Poor Balaam! He had tried to serve two masters and had not succeeded. He had lusted after the riches that Balak offered him, even though it cost him his allegiance to God. He had failed both God and Balak.

But Balaam was not yet finished. God had shamed him before Balak, true, but Balaam had another idea. He might still win the favor of the king. The prophet now sank to his lowest scheming to destroy God's people, upon whom he had pronounced God's blessings.

According to Numbers 31:15 and 16, Balaam counseled Balak how the Moabites might yet gain an advantage over

Israel. "Send the daughters of Moab and Midian to the camp of Israel," he may have said, "to tempt their men to sin."

Balaam's plan worked, just as he had hoped it would. Before long, the men of Israel had committed whoredom and were even worshiping the idols of Moab.

In the Book of Revelation, there is a reference to Balaam, "Who taught Balak to cast a stumbling block before the children of Israel, to eat things sacrificed unto idols, and to commit fornication."[3]

At last Balaam had gained favor with the Moabites and the Midianites. At last he had satisfied his heart's desire. What he had been unable to do as a prophet, he accomplished by trickery and evil counsel.

But Balaam's days were numbered. God commanded the Israelites to avenge themselves upon Midian. The Israelite army swept victoriously across the land, wiping out the Midianites. Finding Balaam, the fallen prophet, they killed him.

The story of Balaam is a sad story of compromise, covetousness, and cowardice. It is the tale of a man through whom God spoke, but who, in turn, forsook God.

We are warned in the Bible not to act as Balaam did—not to "love the wages of unrighteousness"[1] as he did, not to "run greedily after rewards,"[2] not to hold to "the doctrine of Balaam."[3]

And what is the doctrine of Balaam? The doctrine of compromise—trying to serve both God and the world. It is the idea that we can hold to the right, while loving the wrong, or that we can speak pious words insincerely.

Followers of Balaam claim heavenly mansions, while being perfectly at home in their earthly ones. They pray, "Thy will be done," but refuse to let God have His will in their lives.

They preach fasting, and then sit down to feast. They interpret God's "no" to mean "maybe," and keep on asking "why?"

Certainly, Balaam's sins were many and great. Both his dishonest life and his tragic death are a warning to us.

---

1. 2 Peter 2:15.
2. Jude 11.
3. Revelation 2:14.

CHAPTER SIX

The Sins of Achan

The camp of Israel rang with shouts of gladness. A spirit of rejoicing swept the people. They no longer remembered the struggles and the pain of the wilderness, or their former hopelessness. All these were forgotten now in the sweetness of victory. Jericho had fallen! God had miraculously given the fortified city into their hands. The stone walls had tumbled before the mighty curse of God.

The Israelite army scrambled over the broken ruins, striking down the giants of Jericho as they stood, numb with fear. God commanded Israel to set fire to the city and, as they did so, clouds of black smoke rose skyward. Everything must be destroyed. Only the vessels of silver and gold and brass and iron were to be saved for the treasury of the Lord.

It was Israel's most glorious victory yet. However, even as the cry of the conquerors echoed through the stricken city, something was happening that would bring a sudden end to Israel's joy.

A certain man of the tribe of Judah, Achan, found a beautiful Babylonian garment in a Jericho home.* He looked at it longingly, feeling its rich texture. "What a shame to

---

*The story of Achan is found in Joshua 7.

burn such a fine robe!" he must have thought. "I will keep it for myself."

As Achan hid the garment, his eyes fell upon a pile of silver, and a wedge-shaped piece of gold. These, too, Achan coveted, and he carried the whole lot home to his tent, being careful that no one saw him. Achan buried the stolen goods in the earth beneath his tent.

Achan no doubt convinced himself that what he had done was only reasonable. Surely it was better to make use of the spoils of Jericho than to let them be destroyed. What harm could there be in saving a perfectly good piece of clothing from the flames?

But Achan had committed a grievous sin. He had disobeyed God's command. And his deed brought swift punishment, not only upon himself, but upon the whole nation of Israel.

Israel Hath Sinned

Joshua was Israel's brave leader, and he must have felt pleased with the way God had given Jericho into his hands. Neither he nor any of the other thousands of Israelites knew of Achan's sin. They were both ignorant and innocent of the sin.

And yet, all Israel suffered. As three thousand soldiers of Israel went up to take the small city of Ai, they expected another victory, as at Jericho. God was certainly with them!

How startled they were when the men of Ai came rushing out and beat them back. Israelite soldiers began to fall in the battle. Israel was confused and dismayed. What had happened? Where was the power that had shaken the walls of Jericho from their foundations? As the Israelites fled in disarray, they left 36 dead soldiers on the field.

Joshua fell on his face before the ark of the Lord. He tore his clothes and with the elders of Israel put dust upon his head. He cried out to God, "Why has Israel been defeated?"

The Lord said to Joshua, "Get thee up. Wherefore liest thou thus upon thy face? Israel hath sinned. . . . Neither will I be with you any more, except ye destroy the accursed from among you."

So that was it—*Israel had sinned!* Those were hard words, and Joshua must have been stunned. Who had committed the sin, and in what manner? What was to be done about it?

God told Joshua how to proceed. The next morning, the whole camp came together, having sanctified themselves beforehand. Someone was guilty. Joshua was to cast lots to find out who it was.

Achan must have trembled as all Israel gathered together for the solemn occasion. There was an anxious air as the lots were cast. First, the lot fell on the tribe of Judah. Again, it was cast, and the choice was narrowed to the family of Zerah. Then the lot fell on one household in that family: the household of Zabdi.

Closer and closer came God's accusing finger. Here was Achan's opportunity to break down in repentance and confess tearfully that he had sinned against God, pleading for mercy. But no, Achan remained silent.

Zabdi's household passed silently by, one by one, until the lot fell on Achan. Now there was no escape! The guilty one was discovered. All eyes in Israel turned toward Achan. And still, the man did not speak.

Gently, pleadingly, Joshua said,

> My son, give, I pray thee, glory to the Lord God
> of Israel, and make confession unto him; and tell

me now what thou hast done; hide it not from me (Joshua 7:19).

It was too much. Achan could bear it no longer. His reserve broke, and he confessed,

> Indeed I have sinned against the LORD God of Israel, and thus and thus have I done: When I saw among the spoils a goodly Babylonish garment, and two hundred shekels of silver, and a wedge of gold of fifty shekels weight, then I coveted them, and took them; and, behold, they are hid in the earth in the midst of my tent, and the silver under it (Joshua 7:20, 21).

It was a full confession, though a forced one. Some men ran at once to Achan's tent and came back with the evidence—the stolen goods had been hidden where Achan said they were.

And then followed the sad moment when the penalty for sin was exacted. Achan and all that he possessed—his sons and his daughters, his oxen and his sheep, his tent and all that he had—were taken out to a valley and stoned with stones and burned with fire. Thus was sin put out of the camp of Israel, so that the blessing of God could return to His people.

What lesson can we learn from Achan's failure? Is it that sin cannot be hidden from God? Yes, indeed. But that is not the most important lesson. Is it that sin will be punished? This too is very true, but still, this is not the greatest lesson we learn from Achan.

The story of Achan should not be misunderstood. There is no other story in the Bible that brings out so clearly the lesson we must learn. When there is sin among God's people, it is not merely a problem between God and an individual. It is a problem between God and the whole assembly. Just as Achan's sin among the Israelites cost them God's blessing, so unrepented sin within the church makes it impossible for God's blessings to rest upon a congregation. Among God's people, no man lives unto himself.

It is true that there have been some changes since the days of Achan. In our day, God deals with mankind with a greater spirit of mercy and less with His rod of justice. Yet the consequences of sin are no less serious. Sin is as much a blemish upon God's people as it ever was, and it will bring a reaping. When there is repentance, God is ever ready to pardon and to offer redemption through the shed blood of Christ. But He will not wink at sin, nor overlook disobedience.

In 1 Corinthians 11, the Apostle Paul speaks of preparing for holy communion. Each member of the church is responsible to examine himself to see if he is worthy of the bread and the cup. The entire congregation, under the direction of the ministry, is responsible for dealing with all known sin, purging out the old leaven, that the body of Christ might be pure, "a glorious church, not having spot or wrinkle, or any such thing; but that it should be holy and without blemish."[1]

We need not wonder what would have happened had Israel been unwilling to deal with Achan's sin. God had said clearly, "Neither will I be with you any more, except ye destroy the accursed from among you."

God is always the same holy God, who means what He says. Just as the sin of disobedience brought condemnation to Achan's household, so the sin of disobedience, if not repented of, brings a similar condemnation today. The only way the church can remain pure and untainted is to put the sinner out of the camp. In the Christian church this is done by excommunication.

The lesson of Achan is the lesson that no man among God's people falls or stands by himself. If one man falls, the whole body suffers. There must then follow repentance, or the fallen member has to be separated from the body of Christ.

A little leaven leavens the whole lump. If sin remains in the church, then the whole church will be infected. It will lose its purity, and it will lose God's blessing.

---

1. Ephesians 5:27.

CHAPTER SEVEN

The Sins of Eli, the High Priest

Eli was the high priest, a descendant of Aaron.* The Bible does not tell us much about his early life, but it does tell us quite a bit about his old age, when his sons had taken over many of the priestly duties in the tabernacle.

Eli's story is a sad account of sin in the life of an otherwise righteous man. Eli's error was not in the way he served as priest. He seems to have been an able high priest. His problem was not at the tabernacle but at home. He failed as a father, not fulfilling his duty to his two sons. If any man has the idea that a minister's responsibilities to the church come before his responsibilities to his children, he should study Eli's life.

Two Wicked Sons

The Bible gives us a good description of Eli's sons: Hophni and Phinehas. As sons of the high priest, it fell to them to become priests also and to serve in the tabernacle at Shiloh.

As priests, these young men held positions of influence. They should have been examples to all of Israel, as the people came up to sacrifice at the tabernacle. Theirs was a position

---

*The story of Eli is found in 1 Samuel 1:1–4:18.

of spiritual leadership, a standard that called for men of high moral character.

How did Hophni and Phinehas measure up? They did not. They were not fit to be priests, for they were ungodly men, blasphemers before God. They were dishonest, irreverent, and disrespectful. They sinned willfully, paying no attention when their father rebuked them.

The Bible calls them "sons of Belial," which means that they were worthless, lawless fellows. They knew not the Lord. They stole the best pieces of meat from the sacrifices, and this they did high-handedly, using force to get what they wanted if someone refused to give it to them. On top of this evil, they committed fornication with the women at the door of the tabernacle.

Eli's sons made a mockery of the priesthood. They acted like common criminals and as wickedly as heathens. The Scriptures say, "The sin of the young men was very great before the Lord."

It is not the sin of Eli's sons that should most concern us, however. The question that should bother us is, *Why* were they ungodly men? How did the sons of the high priest grow up to be such outlaws?

What had Eli done wrong? That is the question. Or what had he left undone? In his role as parent and priest, how had he failed? He seems to have been a righteous, kindhearted old man. Why then did God hold him responsible for the sins of his sons?

He Restrained Them Not

God held Eli accountable for the way his sons lived, but in exactly what manner Eli erred is not told us. However, enough is given to us that we can fit together the picture.

Eli did not have his eyes closed to what his sons were doing. And it is not that he did not care. He rebuked them soundly.

> Why do ye such things? he asked. For I hear of your evil dealings from all the people. No, my sons; it is no good report that I hear the people of the Lord spreading abroad. If a man sins against a man, God will mediate for him. But if a man sins against the Lord, who can intercede for him? (1 Samuel 2:23-25, free translation).

This sincere, heartfelt admonition was not enough. Although Eli was troubled by his sons' evil-doings, he was not willing to do what needed to be done. The words he spoke fell short of his full responsibility.

But what could Eli do, if his sons would not listen to him? Were not his hands tied? It is easy to excuse poor old Eli, but that is not the way God saw the matter. God sent a man, a prophet, to speak to Eli, and the words he spoke were hard words indeed. The message was not directed to the wicked sons but to the aged high priest.

> Why do you look with greedy eyes at my sacrifices and my offerings which I commanded, and honor your sons above me by fattening yourselves upon the choicest parts of every offering of my people Israel? (1 Samuel 2:29, free translation).

There was something Eli could have done, and rightly *should* have done. After all, he was the high priest. He might have told his sons,

> This absolutely cannot go on. Even though you are my sons, you are not fit to be the priests of God.

God will not allow it. You must resign. If you refuse, I will call all Israel together, and you will be forced to give your places to someone worthy of the work.

It would not have been easy, but Eli could have done it. It would have been very painful, for they were his own flesh and blood, his own two sons, whom he loved. Yet had his love for God outweighed his love for his sons, he would have done his duty, however much it hurt.

But Eli took the path of least resistance. He told his sons they were doing wrong, but that was as far as he went. When they continued sinning as before, Eli withdrew from the scene and let them do as they pleased. Perhaps he thought, "They are of age. Let them answer to God for themselves."

With time, Eli got used to the situation, and it no longer seemed so evil. The day may have come when Eli himself ate of the meat that his sons had stolen from the offerings. Of this we cannot be absolutely sure, but the prophet's words suggest this was true.

And there came a man of God unto Eli, and said unto him, Thus saith the Lord, Did I plainly appear unto the house of thy father, when they were in Egypt in Pharaoh's house? And did I choose him out of all the tribes of Israel to be my priest, to offer upon mine altar, to burn incense, to wear an ephod before me? and did I give unto the house of thy father all the offerings made by fire of the children of Israel? Wherefore kick ye at my sacrifice and at mine offering, which I have commanded in my habitation; and honourest thy sons above me, to make yourselves fat with the chiefest of all the offerings of Israel my people? (1 Samuel 2:27-29).

The Boy Samuel

In his last days, Eli was glad for a willing young helper to assist him in the work of the tabernacle. This young lad was Samuel. God had already chosen him to be Israel's future prophet and judge.

When the first message from God came to the boy Samuel as he lay alone in his room one night, it was a judgment upon Eli's family.

> For I have told him that I will judge his house forever for the iniquity which he knoweth; because his sons made themselves vile, and he restrained them not. And therefore I have sworn unto the house of Eli, that the iniquity of Eli's house shall not be purged with sacrifice nor offering for ever (1 Samuel 3:13, 14).

The tidings lay heavy on Samuel's young mind. How could he tell Eli what God had said? The old man was like a kind grandfather to him, and Samuel loved him. But in the morning, Eli demanded to know the truth. Samuel told him everything.

Eli listened. Then he said, "It is the Lord. Let him do what seems good to him."

God's punishment was not long delayed. The Philistines came up to war against Israel, and the two armies faced each other on the field. In the first day's battle, the Israelites were driven back.

Then the leaders of Israel made a bold move. They took the Ark of the Lord out of the tabernacle at Shiloh and carried it with them into battle against the Philistines. Perhaps they thought that by some strange power, the Ark would save them from their enemies.

It was a terrible thing to do—to thus misuse the Ark of God. The Israelites would hardly have done it, had they not become hardened by years of disrespect for God's sacrifices.

Who should accompany the Ark to the battlefield? The two sons of Eli, of course. Boldly they took the sacred Ark to the Israelite camp. The soldiers of Israel let out a great shout when the Ark arrived, so that the earth rang with their noise.

With renewed confidence, the army of Israel marched toward their enemies. They would overthrow the Philistines for certain! For in the midst of the Israelite soldiers was the Ark of God. This was the last glimpse we are given of Eli's sons.

Eli went out to the wayside and seated himself upon a stool to wait anxiously for word of the battle. He was ninety-eight years old and nearly blind. His heart trembled for the Ark of God. One cannot help feeling compassion for the old man. He knew well what God had promised to bring to pass upon his family. He realized that he himself was greatly to blame.

Eli waits, and he waits. At last, he hears the noise of shouting, and he knows the news has come. It is not good news. Eli leans forward, trembling, trying to make out the words, and his heart beats faster.

He cannot see, but he hears the rapid footsteps as a messenger runs near.

"How did it go, my son?" gasps Eli.

The messenger cries:

> There hath been also a great slaughter among the people, and thy two sons also, Hophni and Phinehas, are dead, and the ark of God is taken (1 Samuel 4:17).

The old man had sat motionless till he heard the last words, "The Ark of God is taken." These were too much for Eli. He fell off his seat backward and broke his neck.

Thus ended the life of the high priest who failed miserably in his duties as a father. Grieved by the sins of his children, he failed to restrain them as he should have done.

The Sins of King Saul

The Spirit of a King

The prophet Samuel had grown old. He had placed his two rather worthless sons in the position of judges, and they began to take advantage of the people, accepting bribes. This caused widespread dissatisfaction and, at last, the elders of Israel came to Samuel with a request. "Make us a king to judge us," they demanded.*

Samuel was grieved by their request. He attempted to persuade Israel that it was a mistake, but the people refused to listen.

"Nay," they said, "we will have a king over us so that we also may be like all the nations, and that our king may judge us and go out before us and fight our battles."

Then the Lord said to Samuel, "Hearken to their voice and make them a king . . . for they have not rejected you, but they have rejected Me."

Saul first appears in the Scriptures as a farmer's son, searching the countryside for his father's lost donkeys. He and his servant looked in vain. Unable to find the missing animals, they decided to consult Samuel. This was all accord-

---

*The story of King Saul is found in 1 Samuel 8—2 Samuel 1.

ing to God's plan, for the Lord had told Samuel that Saul was coming, and that he would be the king.

When the prophet spoke to Saul, the young man showed commendable humility. "Am I not a Benjaminite, of the smallest of the tribes of Israel?" he asked. "And is not my family the least of all the families of Benjamin? Why do you speak thus to me?" Saul was humble in his own eyes and behaved nobly. In all that he did, we do not detect any flaw in his character.

In a private ceremony, Samuel anointed Saul to be the king of Israel. Before dismissing him, the prophet told Saul of a number of events that would happen on his way home. When these things came to pass, Saul should accept them as a sign that God had indeed chosen him.

One of the signs was that Saul would meet a company of prophets. Then, Samuel explained, "The Spirit of the Lord will come upon you and you shall prophesy with them, and you shall be changed into another man." This came to pass just as Samuel had predicted. Saul did, indeed, prophesy along with the young prophets, and God gave him another heart.

Later, Samuel called all the people together at Mizpeh for an official, public ceremony in which God's choice of king would be announced. One by one, the tribes passed before Samuel, until the tribe of Benjamin was chosen. Then the household of Kish was chosen, and at last the selection narrowed to Saul.

But where was he? The people looked all around, but Saul could not be found. A timid man by nature, Saul had hidden himself from the sight of the people.

They brought him forth, a striking young man who was very handsome and taller by a head than the rest of the people.

Samuel said to Israel, "Do you see whom the Lord has chosen, that there is no one like him among all the people?"

Then a shout arose, "Long live the king!" (NIV)

Saul did not immediately set up his kingdom. Instead, he returned to his father's house and continued his life much as before. But it would not be long before Saul was thrust into leadership.

The king of the Ammonites laid siege against Jabesh-gilead, an Israelite city. The men of Jabesh were willing to accept their lot as servants of the Ammonites and thus to strike a truce. But Nahash, the heathen king, was not easily pacified. It would not be enough if they were merely his servants.

"The only way we can reach an agreement," he declared sadistically, "is if you allow me to gouge out the right eye of every one of you!"

Terrified, the elders of Jabesh sent messengers throughout Israel, begging for someone to come to their rescue. When the word came to Saul's hometown, all the people raised their voices and wept because of the misfortune that was to fall upon their fellow citizens. When Saul came home from the field, he asked, "What is wrong with the people that they are weeping?"

When the situation was explained to Saul, the Spirit of God came upon him, and his anger was greatly aroused. At once, he took a yoke of oxen, killed them and cut them into pieces. He sent the pieces throughout Israel by the hands of messengers. In a true kingly spirit, Saul announced, "Whoever does not go out with Saul and Samuel to battle, so shall it be done to his oxen."

The fear of the Lord fell upon the people and they rallied around Saul. He led his forces against the Ammonite king and soundly defeated the enemy, thus delivering Jabesh-gilead from the threatened mutilation. Saul emerged from battle a victorious and triumphant king, and the people looked to him with respect. They rejoiced that God had given them such a noble king.

In their celebration, the people said to Samuel, "Where are the people now who said earlier, 'Shall Saul rule over us?' Bring them forth that we may put them to death."

But Saul intervened and said, "There shall not a man be put to death this day; for today the Lord hath wrought salvation in Israel."

Thus Saul began his reign well. Not only had he risen courageously against the enemies of Israel, but he had forgiven those who at first had not supported him. With such a gallant beginning, who would have thought that the time would come when King Saul would fall into great sin and be rejected by the Lord who had chosen him?

Saul Falters

King Saul emerged from the skirmish against Ammon as a national hero. It brought great joy to Israel to think that God had given them such a fine king. But Saul's record was not to remain unblemished for long.

Saul had been reigning over Israel for only two years when the next major crisis arose. Israel's long-time enemy, the Philistines, once again mustered their forces to bring the Israelites into fuller subjection. With thousands of chariots and horsemen, and foot-soldiers as many as the sand on the seashore, the Philistines intimidated Israel even before the battle began.

To tighten their hold upon Israel, the Philistines controlled the making and sharpening of iron. Only Saul and

Jonathan had swords and spears, and without blacksmiths there was no way to fashion additional weapons for the Israelite men. Even if someone needed an axe sharpened or a plowshare repaired, he was forced to take the tool to a Philistine blacksmith. The Israelites no doubt had bows and slings, but what were they against the armed might of the Philistines?

Under such conditions, King Saul had a hard time keeping up the morale of his soldiers. They began gradually to desert him, creeping stealthily away and hiding themselves in the cliffs and caves and thickets of the land. A few even fled across the Jordan to greater safety.

Even those soldiers who faithfully clung to Saul trembled in their sandals. What was the king to do? Samuel had promised to come to Gilgal within seven days, and so Saul waited impatiently for the prophet's arrival. Samuel would offer a sacrifice and seek the Lord's direction.

The week dragged by, one day after another, and still Samuel did not come. Surely he had not forgotten the appointment! Perhaps he had been captured by the Philistines. Meanwhile, the trickle of deserting soldiers increased. There were signs that the Philistines were just about ready to attack. Oh, why did Samuel not come? For Saul, the situation had reached a critical stage.

During the seventh day, Saul grew desperate. Under the severe pressure of the moment, his true character began to show. "Bring a burnt offering to me," he commanded, "and peace offerings." For him to proceed on his own was unlawful, but King Saul had reached his limit. Perhaps he reasoned that it was better to offer a sacrifice unlawfully than not to sacrifice at all. Surely, his course was the lesser of two evils.

The smoke had barely died down when the prophet Samuel appeared. If only Saul had waited a little longer! But now the deed was done, and there was no undoing it.

The king hurried toward Samuel to greet him, as if he had done no wrong. Samuel asked him, "What have you done?"

Saul launched into a lengthy justification of his actions.

> I saw that my people were scattering. You didn't come as soon as you had said. The Philistines were just about to come down upon us, and I had not yet made supplication to the Lord. So I felt compelled to offer a burnt offering (1 Samuel 13:11, 12, paraphrased).

There, it all sounded so reasonable. Surely Samuel would understand. Who could blame Saul? Because of the circumstances he had been forced to do something. . . .

But Samuel was not understanding at all. "You have done foolishly," he said to Saul. "You have not kept the commandment of the Lord your God."

Samuel went on to explain, "Therefore, the kingdom that was yours will be given to another—to someone more worthy!"

Saul had failed his first major test. Had he been faithful, the kingdom would have remained in his family for generations. But he had sinned against God.

A Second Chance

Several years passed before King Saul was again put to the test. It almost seems as if God wanted to give him a second chance to provide the spiritual leadership that Israel needed, a second opportunity to prove himself and be true to God's command.

Years earlier, while Moses still lived, God had said to the Israelites,

> Remember what Amalek did unto thee by the way, when ye were come forth out of Egypt; how he met thee by the way, and smote the hindmost of thee, even all that were feeble behind thee, when thou wast faint and weary; and he feared not God.
>
> Therefore it shall be, when the LORD thy God hath given thee rest from all thine enemies round about, in the land which the LORD thy God giveth thee for an inheritance to possess it, that thou shalt blot out the remembrance of Amalek from under heaven; thou shalt not forget it (Deuteronomy 25:17-29).

The time was ripe for judgment upon Amalek, a people that were an abomination to the Lord. It was a time of comparative rest for Israel, whose army had gained recent victories over enemy nations. King Saul's troops no longer consisted of a mere 600 trembling men, but they had grown to an impressive force of more than two hundred thousand.

Samuel brought the word of the Lord to Saul, "Go and smite Amalek and utterly destroy all that they have and spare them not." According to the instructions, not even their livestock should be left alive—all must be slain.

So Saul led his army against the cities of Amalek. The attack went well. Saul smote the Amalekites and thoroughly defeated them. God blessed Israel's efforts with great success.

Now came Saul's opportunity to vindicate himself and to make amends for his former unfaithfulness. But no, once again the king encountered a serious test. Difficult circumstances rose up before him. He was forced to make a crucial choice. Would he obey God's command in full, or would he choose an easier, more permissive way?

King Saul and his men came home from the battle, flushed with victory. But they did not come empty-handed. They brought back with them the spoils of war—fatted calves and the best of the sheep and, in addition, Agag king of Amalek as a captive.

The word of the Lord came to Samuel: "It repenteth me that I have set up Saul to be king: For he is turned back from following me, and hath not performed my commandments."

Samuel was grieved to the heart. He could not sleep that night, for he cried out to the Lord in unceasing prayer. Very early the next morning he set out to find Saul.

Samuel caught up with the king about fifteen miles away at Gilgal. Once again Saul seemed eager to see the aged prophet. Saul spoke first, "Blessed be thou of the Lord! I have performed the commandment of the Lord."

Perhaps it was at that very moment that the penned-up livestock began to bawl. We can hear the irony in Samuel's words as he said to Saul, "What meaneth then this bleating of the sheep in mine ears, and the lowing of the oxen which I hear?"

Oh, but there was an explanation for that! Quick to plead his innocence, Saul explained, "The people spared the best of the sheep and the oxen to sacrifice to the Lord your God. The rest we have utterly destroyed."

Here was a two-pronged denial of guilt. First, Saul laid the blame on someone else. And then, he reasoned that the animals had been kept for a good purpose, a religious purpose, as an offering to the Lord.

Samuel would hear none of it. "Stay!" he said to Saul. "Let me tell you what the Lord said to me last night."

"Say on," answered Saul.

> When you were little in your own eyes, the Lord anointed you to be king over Israel. Now the Lord sent you to destroy the Amalekites. Why did you not obey the voice of the Lord? Why did you swoop down on the spoil and do evil in the sight of the Lord? (1 Samuel 15:17-19, free translation).

Saul was not about to back down. Could the prophet not understand why things had gone the way they had? Surely Samuel could be made to understand. So Saul repeated his story.

> "I have obeyed the voice of the Lord," he insisted. "I brought back Agag, king of Amalek. I have utterly destroyed the Amalekites. But the *people* took the plunder, sheep and oxen, the best of the things to sacrifice to the Lord your God" (1 Samuel 15:20, free translation).

Perhaps the people had done just what Saul said. But Saul, as king, should have given them firm direction, instead of weakly letting them have their way. Was their motive to save the animals for sacrifice? Or was this a pious cover-up—an afterthought once the deed had been done?

Whose idea had it been to bring back King Agag alive? For this, Saul did not try to blame others, but he attempted to make light of it. King Saul likely could not resist the temptation to bring home the enemy king as a trophy of war. But God was not about to accept Saul's reasoning.

With just a few words, the prophet went to the heart of the matter. "Has the Lord as great delight in burnt offerings and sacrifices as in obeying the voice of the Lord?" he asked. Then he answered his own question, "Behold, to obey is better than sacrifice, and to hearken than the fat of rams."

Samuel confronted King Saul with the enormity of his sin. "Rebellion is as the sin of witchcraft," he said, "and stubbornness is as iniquity and idolatry. Because thou hast rejected the word of the LORD, He hath also rejected thee from being king."

The arrow had reached its mark. Saul exclaimed, "I have sinned." Yet, it was not the cry of a penitent man but of one who cringed before the awful consequences of his misdeed. "I have sinned," Saul confessed, "because I feared the people and obeyed their voice. Now therefore, I pray thee, pardon my sin, and turn again with me, that I may worship the LORD."

Samuel saw clearly through Saul's insincerity. He knew that the king's repentance was not genuine, and so he turned away. Saul in his anguish laid hold of the prophet's robe, and it tore in his hands.

Samuel turned upon Saul, "The Lord has rent the kingdom of Israel from you this day and has given it to a neighbor of yours who is better than you are."

No Inward Strength

What was Saul's sin? Can we learn from the mistakes he made?

Above all, of course, Saul was disobedient. But there are many ways to be disobedient. There are various roads leading to reluctant, partial conformity like Saul's. How did Saul arrive there? What will keep us from following in his steps?

Whatever it was that Saul lacked, he was not a strong character who could stand up under pressure. He lacked the inner resources of a true leader of God's people. When Saul got into a tight spot, he sought the easy way out. He was a man readily influenced by others.

In this, King Saul was no different from most of us. It is a common human trait to be swayed by popular opinion. It is not easy to go against others' wishes, especially when it threatens our ego. The price of total commitment to God is high, and our flesh shrinks from the sacrifice.

Saul's tragedy was magnified because he was no ordinary man—he was the king. It was his responsibility to make the right decisions and then to abide by them, even against strong opposition. It was his duty to set a standard to influence others, to be a leader and not a follower.

Similarly today, ministers have been ordained to provide leadership for God's people, to teach God's Word, and to hold up the standard of truth. How often we observe entire churches apostasizing because the ministers have failed to uphold the Lord's standard. The walls of separation between the church and the world crumble, because there is no clear vision that God's people are set apart as a holy people.

The power to discipline erring members has been lost. There is little respect for authority or church leadership. There is much verbal admonition and pious talk, but very little serious discipleship.

The final twist, of course, is to find religious excuses for our disobedience. It is not hard to discover them. Anyone with a bit of imagination can find a religious reason for his disobedience. That is what Saul did. Naturally, no one is going to admit that he is covering up, or that his motives are not pure, even as Saul was not willing to admit that selfish greed was the real reason he had spared the sheep and oxen.

A Tragic End

Because Saul had rejected the Lord, the Lord rejected him. He was alienated from God, and one sin followed the other. This set the pattern for the sad remainder of Saul's life.

No sin was more tragic than Saul's burning jealousy toward David, his rival for the throne. Between Saul's fits of despondency and his raging jealousy, there could not have been many happy moments.

Saul had been king of Israel for nearly 40 years. Once more the Philistine armies were arrayed against Israel, determined to invade the land. The prophet Samuel was no longer living. Saul was completely unnerved by the advent of the enemy.

In his despair, the king fasted all day. Then, under the cover of darkness, he made his way to the witch of Endor to seek counsel. Oh, the depth to which King Saul had fallen!

The very next day the king and his three sons died on the battlefield at Gilboa. Thus came to a sorrowful end a life that had begun brilliantly, but had turned bitter because of disobedience.

Saul's greatest test had come the day he fought against Amalek. He failed that test miserably. Is not Amalek symbolic of our own flesh and blood, the nature within us that is inclined to evil? Is not this every Christian's greatest test—to bring into subjection the Amalek within, to submit one's life unreservedly to Christ?

In the New Testament, the Apostle Paul calls us to "crucify the flesh with the affections and lusts."[1] He speaks of "being dead indeed unto sin, but alive unto God through Jesus Christ our Lord."[2] As Christians we are to put to death the inclination to sin that lurks within our flesh. We must not spare even Agag, the most cherished bosom sin, but hew him to pieces before the Lord. For many of us, Agag stands for self-gratification. To spare him is to be lenient with ourselves, to make excuses, to twist God's Word in our own favor, to be less than obedient.

If we fail to give our all to the Lord, we fall into the sin of King Saul. He was quite willing to obey God halfway but rebelled against giving Him all. If we are like Saul, our lives, too, will end in dismal failure.

How startling that at the very end Saul perished on the field of Gilboa at the hand of an Amalekite![3]

---

1. Galatians 5:24.
2. Romans 6:11.
3. See 2 Samuel 1.

CHAPTER NINE

The Sin for Which Uzzah Died

The ox cart had never been used before. The smooth wood glistened brightly in the morning sun as the yoke of oxen plodded along the hilly road toward Jerusalem. But the oxen were not alone on the journey. Thousands of people thronged the roadside, some surging ahead of the oxen, some crowding in close behind them. There was the glad sound of musical instruments being played and singing and rejoicing. It was the day the Ark of God was being taken by King David to its new home.*

After many years of fleeing the wrath of Saul, David had at last come into the reign that had been promised him by the prophet Samuel. One of the first concerns of the new king was to bring the Ark of God back to a place of honor and worship.

"If it seems good to you," King David said to all the congregation of Israel, "and if you think it is the Lord's will, let us send and bring the Ark of God to us."

The people agreed. On the appointed day, thousands of men from all parts of Israel gathered with King David at Kir-

---

*The story of Uzzah is found in 2 Samuel 6:1—7; 1 Chronicles 13, 15.

jath-jearim, where the Ark of God had been lodged for many years in the home of Abinadab, a Levite. There, Abinadab's family had cared for the sacred Ark.

We do not know who planned the celebration that day, nor who decided how the procession was to be conducted. This may well have been King David's responsibility, but two of Abinadab's sons, Uzzah and Ahio, played a prominent role in transporting the Ark to its new location.

The Ark of God was placed on a brand new cart built especially for the occasion. Two oxen were hitched to the cart. Ahio took his place in front of the oxen, the best position from which to guide them on their way. But Uzzah's role may have been even more important—he walked alongside the Ark.

All went well for some time. The crowd was in high spirits. The procession moved steadily toward Jerusalem. The distance was not great, about ten miles. But suddenly, there was an abrupt halt. The oxen stumbled. The cart lurched, and the precious Ark of God tipped. Uzzah reached up quickly with his hand to steady the Ark. The moment his fingers touched the Ark, he stiffened and fell to the ground, a lifeless body. Clearly, God had judged Uzzah.

King David was very much distressed. He immediately called a halt to the day's plans. The Ark of God would proceed no further. It was quietly moved into the nearby house of Obed-edom. The subdued crowd began to disperse, the dead man was buried, and people went to their homes in Israel that evening greatly sobered by what had occurred. Why had Uzzah died?

God's Instructions Concerning the Ark

The Ark had been built more than four hundred years before, while the children of Israel were camped near Mount

Sinai.[1] When Moses came down from the mountain with the tablets of stone, God commanded the Israelites to build a sanctuary or tabernacle. Central to the tabernacle was the Ark of God, in which the tablets containing the Ten Commandments were to be placed.

God was specific about how the Ark was to be built—the dimensions, the materials to be used, and its design. The Ark was to be overlaid inside and out with gold. The two cherubim faced each other, and between them was the mercy seat—the site from which God's presence would commune with Moses and the Israelites. The Ark of God was the center of Israel's worship.

God was just as specific about how the Ark was to be moved from place to place. Two staves were to be inserted through rings on each side, and these staves were never to be removed. With these, the Ark was to be carried on the shoulders of four priests. Not just any priests, but the Kohathites, a branch of the Levites, were to carry the Ark. They were warned never to touch the Ark, lest they die.

What Was Uzzah's Sin?

We may question who was responsible for the tragedy that occurred during the Ark's transportation to Jerusalem. All the priests should have known better than to move the Ark on an ox cart.

Surely King David was aware that God had commanded that the Ark be moved only on the shoulders of four Levites of the house of Kohath.

What about Uzzah? He, too, must have known these things. He must have known that it was forbidden even for the priests to touch the Ark.

If these facts were known, why did no one speak up when the new ox cart was brought forth and the Ark loaded upon it? Perhaps they all may have reasoned that an ox cart had worked well for the Philistines (1 Samuel 6:7). Why not use another cart? Surely God would be pleased with this shiny, new, custom-made cart to carry His Ark.

We do not know how much Uzzah knew, nor what his thoughts were. Yet the fact that God's anger was kindled against him when he touched the Ark shows that God held Uzzah accountable, and that Uzzah was not without sin.

Uzzah may have reasoned that he would not touch the Ark unless it was necessary. But if an emergency should occur, it would be better to transgress one little command than to allow the Ark to crash to the ground.

Perhaps we are being too hard on Uzzah. And yet, there is evidence that he was guilty of more than an unpremeditated touching of the Ark. He must have known that an ox cart was not God's approved way of transporting the Ark. God would not have struck down Uzzah unless Uzzah was guilty of a serious sin.

Although Uzzah died there beside the ox cart so many years ago and his body has long been buried, the spirit that motivated him has survived to the present day. Human nature has not changed. The temptations that brought Uzzah to an untimely death are temptations that come to Christians today, though in a variety of new forms.

True, in our day of grace, God is not likely to strike men dead as He struck down Uzzah. Yet, when men ignore God's clear commands and replace them with human reasoning or seek to follow worldly examples, God's judgment still takes its course. Great blessings are lost, and in their place curses come. God is not mocked. Whatever a man sows, that a man also reaps.[2] What great suffering and sin have resulted, when men and women have bent God's Word to their own liking!

In our day many people choose to ignore clear Biblical teachings, or they go to great pains to reason them away. There are human methods of confusing and muddling God's laws and reshaping them to fit our preferences. There are ways of seeing what we *want* to see and hearing what we *want* to hear. There are means of twisting the Scriptures to our own destruction.[3]

Today we are not tempted to fashion new ox carts for moving that which God intended to be carried by His special priests. But the same spirit causes us to evade the full import of New Testament teachings.

Consider Christian marriage. God's original intention at Creation was that marriage be the lifelong union of one man and one woman, to be dissolved only upon the death of one of them. Jesus restored marriage to this standard.[4] In our generation, we have seen wholesale erosion of God's concept of marriage. Marriage is not the same as it was a hundred, or even fifty, years ago. Vows are made light of, until even respectable people divorce and remarry at will. In addition, it has become common for unmarried people to live together as if they were married.

Has this "moral revolution" had an impact upon us as well? Does marriage retain the degree of sacredness and permanence in the believers' eyes that it once had? Or has the world's way influenced our thinking?

The spirit of Uzzah's generation would dull our consciences to God's Word and have us copy the example of those who do not believe. Because we are so widely exposed to the loose morals of our day and hear the free talk and read the viewpoints of those who disregard God's Word, we may eventually be blinded to the clear teachings of the Bible. This is alarming.

I remember my grandmother relating an incidence of immorality in the youth group of which she was a member years ago. The whole church wept and mourned as if at a funeral. However, today, in that same community, the sin which once caused deep grieving has become commonplace and accepted. And yet, the Apostle Paul clearly taught that fornication and all uncleanness should not once be named among Christians.[5]

Consider also the Biblical role of husband and wife. The New Testament teaches unmistakably that the husband is the head of the wife, even as Christ is the head of the church,[6] and that he should love his wife as Christ loved the church.[7] Although a husband and wife are "heirs together of the grace of life,"[8] yet the man is given leadership and authority. He has the greater responsibility. Nevertheless, he is not to lord it over his wife but to give her due consideration as the weaker vessel and not to be bitter against her.[9]

The wife is instructed to "submit to her own husband as unto the Lord." As the church is subject unto Christ, a wife is to be subject to her own husband in everything.[10] She is to reverence her husband, to love and be obedient to him, bearing children, guiding the house, and giving no occasion for reproach.[11] Her adorning is not to be outward, but "the ornament of a meek and quiet spirit."[12] She is to be silent in the church, and if she would learn anything, she is to ask her husband at home.[13]

Few subjects are more clearly taught in the New Testament than the distinct roles of husband and wife. In spite of the clarity of God's Word, however, many people in our day pay little attention. Popular thinking wants to equalize the roles of men and women—"liberating" women from being suppressed. The Biblical pattern of leadership and authority is flatly rejected. Family responsibility becomes a fifty-fifty arrangement. Women are allowed to lead congregations and to preach.

Arguments for change sound so reasonable and fair. And yet it is a far cry from what the Bible teaches.

In the parent-child relationship we have another clear authority pattern in the Scriptures. It is a responsibility of Christian parents to bring up their children in the nurture and admonition of the Lord, not with a heavy hand but with true parental love, lest they provoke the children to wrath or bitterness.[14]

Children, in turn, are commanded to obey their parents and to honor them. The fifth of the Ten Commandments is renewed and reinforced by the Apostle Paul.

> Children, obey your parents in the Lord: for this is right. Honor thy father and mother; (which is the first commandment with promise;) that it may be well with thee, and thou mayest live long on the earth (Ephesians 6:1, 2).

How very clear! And yet, how widely ignored! Too often parents fail in their parental duty—they allow their children to have their own way from babyhood on. Children do not learn to submit their wills and be obedient. In such a permissive setting, it is no wonder children are rebellious and have no respect for authority.

But the fault does not always lie entirely with the parents. A rebellious spirit is like a contagious disease, especially if it is fanned by peer pressure. This rebellion will even adopt religious tones, turning the commandment in Ephesians 6:1 completely on end. Paul said it is the child's duty to obey his parents "in the Lord." Defiant teenagers extract the opposite meaning—they do not need to obey their parents because what the parents request is not, in the child's opinion, "in the Lord." Modern-day Uzzahs who are not willing to follow the Scriptures!

A true Christian love for another is clearly taught in the New Testament. Can anyone mistake the Apostle John's message in his first epistle?

> If a man say, I love God, and hateth his brother, he is a liar: for he that loveth not his brother whom he hath seen, how can he love God whom he hath not seen? And this commandment have we from him, that he who loveth God love his brother also (1 John 4:20, 21).

> By this we know that we love the children of God, when we love God, and keep his commandments. For this is the love of God, that we keep his commandments: and his commandments are not grievous (1 John 5:2, 3).

Here we touch the very heart of many church problems. We do well to examine ourselves. How do we measure up? What does God think of our love for our brother? If a man truly loves God, he will love his brother. And the way we can know that we really love our brother is that we keep God's commandments. That, according to John, is the telltale evidence—obedience.

Uzzah did not obey. Because of his disobedience, he died beside the road. No doubt, the account of his death is written for our warning. How can we learn from his mistakes? What are the temptations facing us today? Are they similar to those that led to Uzzah's death?

1. Exodus 25:10-22; 37:1-9; Numbers 3:27-32; 4:15; 7:1-9.
2. Galatians 6:7.
3. 2 Peter 3:16.
4. Matthew 19:3-6.
5. Ephesians 5:3.
6. Ephesians 5:23; 1 Corinthians 11:1-16.
7. Ephesians 5:23, 33.
8. 1 Peter 3:7.
9. Colossians 3:19; 1 Peter 3:7.
10. Ephesians 5:22, 24; Colossians 3:18; 1 Peter 3:1, 5.
11. Ephesians 5:33; Titus 2:4, 5.
12. 1 Timothy 2:9-11; 1 Peter 3:3-5.
13. 1 Corinthians 14:34, 35; 1 Timothy 2:11, 12.
14. Ephesians 6:4; Colossians 3:21.

CHAPTER TEN

King David's Grave Sin

By the time David* came to the throne of Israel, he had already survived harrowing experiences. As a shepherd, he had faced a lion and a bear, slaying them both. With five stones and a sling he had ventured forth against the heavily-armed giant Goliath. He had dodged King Saul's javelins and fled from the jealous king's hatred, hiding in the wilderness of Judea.

Through the many perils of his turbulent life, David had been preserved from death. God's hand had been on him and shielded him again and again. God's hand, too, had brought David to the throne of Israel. God had given David victory over his enemies. In a series of wars, David extended the borders of Israel. At last, David reigned over a powerful, influential nation.

King David was a gifted and talented man: a skilled musician possessed of a poetic soul unsurpassed in Israel. The poet-king was a deep thinker, a pious man, whose many psalms were divinely inspired.

What of flaws in David's character? As a young man David showed evidence of few. As he established his kingdom and made Jerusalem his royal city, there was little for which he could justly be criticized.

---

*This story of King David is found in 2 Samuel 11—12:24; Psalm 51.

There was one notable exception. Early, David took multiple wives for himself in violation of God's commandments for the kings of Israel. At first thought, such a lapse might seem of minor importance in comparison with the total success of David's life. However, as events unfolded in David's life, this lapse suddenly stands out in bold relief.

A Fateful Evening

David was no longer a young man. He was, perhaps, about 50 years old. His fortune and fame had grown, as had the size of the royal household. His many wives bore him sons and daughters. They grew up accustomed to the privileges of their position in life.

It was the spring of the year: the time when kings go forth to battle. King David, however, did not go out to battle that spring. He sent his commander Joab at the head of the army of Israel to fight, while the king remained in his palace, at ease.

There is an old proverb, proven and true, that "idleness is the devil's workshop." Where men should be at work but spend their time loitering, they often fall into sin. David had been resting on his cot one afternoon, perhaps to escape the sultry heat. As the cool evening breezes began to stir, the king rose from his bed. The daylight lingered. The king walked upon the rooftop, and his eyes looked down upon a woman who was washing herself. Even from a distance, David could see that she was a beautiful woman.

Then the king did what he should not have done—he sent a messenger to find out who this woman was. The returning messenger said, "Is it not Bathsheba, the wife of Uriah the Hittite?" That should have arrested David's curiosity. Bathsheba was a married woman. Her husband Uriah was an officer in the king's army. He was off fighting for Israel. But David took a fateful step—he sent for Bathsheba.

Many centuries later the Apostle James wrote,

> Every man is tempted, when he is drawn away of his own lust, and enticed. Then when lust hath conceived, it bringeth forth sin: and sin, when it is finished, bringeth forth death (James 1:14, 15).

A few minutes of fleshly indulgence marred King David's character. The peace of his conscience was destroyed, his kingdom was placed in great peril, and an occasion was given to his enemies to blaspheme the Lord.

However, the sordid story is not finished. Worse is yet to come. David tried to cover his sin. It must not become known!

After some time, a startling message came to King David from his partner in sin—she was with child. Her condition could not long be hidden. If the deed became known, David's honor would be wracked by scandal. Besides, the Law of Moses required that both parties in adultery should be stoned to death. Something would have to be done.

David moved into action. Uriah the officer was called from the battlefield on the pretense that King David wanted to know how the war was faring. Uriah came dutifully and answered the king's questions. Then the king sent him home to his wife. But the noble Uriah refused.

> The ark, and Israel, and Judah, abide in tents; and my lord Joab, and the servants of my lord, are encamped in the open fields; shall I then go into mine house, to eat and to drink, and to lie with my wife? as thou livest, and as thy soul liveth, I will not do this thing (2 Samuel 11:11).

So he slept in the king's porch and refused to go to his own home.

David took another tack. The next day, he dined Uriah and made him drunk. Once more he tried to send the Hittite home. Brave Uriah held to his resolve.

The king's attempt to cover his sin had been foiled. The desperate king became even more desperate. His awful sin gouged deeper into David's character. David imagined only one way to save face. He must get rid of Uriah! Dead men tell no tales.

The treachery that David then embraced has seldom been equaled. In desperation and guilt, David wrote a letter to Joab, commander of his army. The letter was Uriah's death warrant, signed by the king. David dispatched the letter by the victim's own hand.

"Set Uriah in the front line where the battle is hottest," David wrote. "Then draw back from him so that he may be smitten and die."

On the battlefield, Joab asked no questions. He hastened to obey the king's instructions. The sinister plot unfolded without a catch. Uriah, always valiant and loyal, ever true to his superiors, fell, mortally wounded.

In the aftermath, Joab played the game according to the king's rules. He dispatched a messenger at once, saying, "If the king is angry that there have been losses, and if he asks what we were doing so near to the city wall, tell him that his servant Uriah the Hittite is dead."

King David listened to the messenger's report. His was the response of a tortured conscience, momentarily relieved to hear that his scheme had worked.

"Tell Joab," David told the courier, "that he must not let this displease him. The sword devoureth one as well as another. Tell him to press on in his battle against the city and to overthrow it."

When Bathsheba heard that her husband was dead, she mourned for him. When the customary week of mourning was past, David sent for her. She came to his own house and became his wife. The baby that would be born would come into the world as a legitimate child, outwardly within the requirements of the law.

But the thing that David had done displeased the Lord.

The Little Ewe Lamb

The Bible does not tell us what happened during the months that followed David's great sin. Did he toss on his pillow at night, regretting he had ever given in to the temptation? Did apparitions of Uriah rise up in his dreams to torment him?

As the day approached that the child should be born, the Lord sent a prophet to speak to the king. Nathan began by telling a story.

There were two men in a city. The one was a rich man and the other poor. The rich man had many flocks and herds, but the poor man had only one little ewe lamb. He raised the little lamb in his own house and nourished it. It grew up with his children, ate his food, drank from his cup, lay in his bosom, and was just like a daughter to him.

One day a traveler came to the rich man's house. Rather than taking a lamb from his own flock, the rich man came to the poor man's house. He seized the little pet ewe lamb and killed it to serve to his guest (2 Samuel 12:1-4, free translation).

As Nathan fell silent, David became very angry. "As the LORD liveth," he exclaimed to Nathan, "the man that hath done this thing shall surely die!"

Nathan looked directly into David's eyes and said, "Thou art the man!"

Then the prophet rebuked him.

> Wherefore hast thou despised the commandment of the LORD, to do evil in his sight? thou hast killed Uriah the Hittite with the sword, and hast taken his wife to be thy wife, and hath slain him with the sword of the children of Ammon. Now therefore the sword shall never depart from thine house; because thou hast despised me, and hast taken the wife of Uriah the Hittite to be thy wife (2 Samuel 12:9, 10).

How David's head must have fallen upon his breast as the prophet continued to speak! The king had sinned, and now he must give account for his sin. God would not hold him guiltless. There would follow a terrible reaping. Nathan finished:

> Thus saith the LORD, Behold, I will raise up evil against thee out of thine own house, and I will take thy wives before thine eyes, and give them unto thy neighbor, and he shall lie with thy wives in the sight of this sun. For thou didst it secretly: but I will do this thing before all Israel, and before the sun (2 Samuel 12:11, 12).

What could David say? Only six words, "I have sinned against the LORD."

For nearly a year the wound had festered, the guilt had built up pressure, and the pain had gnawed at David's heart. Now in one, short, heartfelt confession, David's sore burst, and the cleansing, healing process began. *I have sinned against the Lord.* The guilty one was tired of hiding. He was weary of running. A sigh of relief must have flooded those words, "I, [David], have sinned against the LORD."

How sweet to hear the response: "The LORD also hath put away thy sin. Thou shalt not die!"

David deserved to die. He had broken no fewer than three of the Ten Commandments, perhaps four. The death penalty was his just due. Yet God saw that David's repentance was sincere. He graciously granted David a pardon. However, there would be a grim reaping. David's life would never again be the same.

Still, immediate consequences could not be avoided. "Because by this deed thou hast given great occasion to the enemies of the LORD to blaspheme," Nathan concluded, "the child also that is born unto thee shall surely die."

The parents who had sinned would live, but the innocent child born of their sin must die!

> O the depth of the riches both of the wisdom and knowledge of God! How unsearchable are his judgments, and his ways past finding out! For who hath known the mind of the Lord? Or who hath been his counsellor? (Romans 11:33, 34).

A Penitent's Prayer

The prophet departed, leaving David and Bathsheba to think upon his words. The baby fell gravely ill, sick unto death. The veil had been torn away from David's eyes, and he could see the situation in all of its stark reality. David had sinned grievously against the Lord, but the innocent child would suffer.

David fasted, lying all night upon the ground in prayer and penitence. The elders of his house came to him, seeking to raise him up, but he would not. He would not eat the food that they brought to him. David's sorrow was deep, deep remorse for his sins.

It seems likely during this time that David wrote the poignant words of the 51st Psalm:

> Have mercy upon me, O God, according to thy loving kindness: according unto the multitude of thy tender mercies blot out my transgressions.
>
> Wash me throughly from mine iniquity, and cleanse me from my sin. For I acknowledge my transgressions: and my sin is ever before me. . . .
>
> Purge me with hyssop, and I shall be clean: wash me, and I shall be whiter than snow. Make me to hear joy and gladness; that the bones which thou hast broken may rejoice. Hide thy face from my sins, and blot out all mine iniquities. Create in me a clean heart, O God; and renew a right spirit within me. Cast me not away from thy presence; and take not thy holy spirit from me. . . .
>
> Deliver me from blood-guiltiness, O God, thou God of my salvation: and my tongue shall sing aloud of thy righteousness. O Lord, open thou my lips; and my mouth shall show forth thy praise.
>
> For thou desirest not sacrifice; else would I give it: thou delightest not in burnt offering. The

sacrifices of God are a broken spirit: a broken and a contrite heart, O God, thou wilt not despise.

David cried to the Lord for seven days, and on the seventh day the child died. David's servants were afraid to tell the king. If David had mourned so greatly while the baby was ill, how would he respond when he learned the child was dead?

Hearing his servants whispering, David asked, "Is the child dead?"

"He is dead," they replied.

David rose from the ground. He washed and anointed himself, changed his clothes, and came to the house of the Lord to worship. Afterwards, he returned to his own house and asked for bread.

The servants were perplexed. They said to David,

> Thou didst fast and weep for the child, while it was alive; but when the child was dead, thou didst rise and eat bread. And he said, While the child was yet alive, I fasted and wept: for I said, Who can tell whether GOD will be gracious to me, that the child may live? But now he is dead, wherefore should I fast? can I bring him back again? I shall go to him, but he shall not return to me (2 Samuel 12:22, 23).

Although David's sin was forgiven, it cast a dark shadow over the remaining years of his life. The prophet Nathan's prediction came true. David's household was wracked by open scandal, and the sword was never far removed. David's own sons rose up to wrest the kingdom from their father, but did not succeed.

When his son Absalom was killed while trying to overthrow his father's rule, King David would not be comforted. He cried,

"O my son Absalom, my son, my son Absalom! would to God that I had died for thee, O Absalom, my son, my son!"

Why was the cry so bitter? Was it not that David, in Absalom's tragic death, saw once again the consequences of his own great sin? His son had been slain, but it was David who deserved to die. In the end, no fewer than four of David's sons died violently in the backlash of his grave sin.

Yet, not *all* was sorrow in David's later years. God blessed the king and Bathsheba with another son, whom they named Solomon. In a measure they were comforted. The dark cloud had been pierced by a ray of hope for the future.

CHAPTER ELEVEN

The Sins of the Wisest Man

Danger like a storm cloud hung over young Solomon's head as the time came for a new king to be crowned in Israel. David lay on his bed dying, a feeble old man no longer capable of running the affairs of the nation. Earlier David had made known his choice of a successor—Solomon, son of Bathsheba.*

Not everyone in Israel was enthused by David's choice, nor were they willing to wait until the old king died. An older son, Adonijah, felt he had a greater right to the throne than Solomon. In his claim he had the support of several powerful men in Israel, especially Joab, the commander of David's army, and Abiathar, the priest. Secretly, Adonijah rallied his forces. He planned a feast outside of Jerusalem and invited a large number of key men. The purpose of the feast was clear to all those who attended. Adonijah was making a bid for the kingdom. He was exalting himself, saying, "I will be king."

When news of the ominous gathering reached Jerusalem, the prophet Nathan became alarmed. He quickly sent Bathsheba to the bedside of the king to tell him what Adonijah was doing. As Bathsheba spoke to David, the prophet came in and confirmed her report.

---

*The story of King Solomon is found in 1 Kings 1–11; 2 Chronicles 1–9.

"My lord, O king," Nathan said to David, "hast thou said, 'Adonijah shall reign after me, and he shall sit upon my throne'?"

Though David was weak and bedfast, he realized the seriousness of the situation. He ordered that Solomon be proclaimed the new king of Israel at once. Solomon was placed on King David's mule and led through the streets of Jerusalem. Zadok the priest anointed Solomon. Trumpets were blown, and all the people cried out, "God save King Solomon!" The whole city rang with rejoicing.

The sounds of Solomon's coronation reached the ears of Adonijah and his supporters, and they panicked. The guests dispersed, fleeing for their lives. Adonijah fled to the altar and caught hold of the horns, hoping to find asylum there.

A Wise Young King

Before David died, he gave his blessing and counsel to the young King Solomon.

> Keep the charge of the LORD thy God, to walk in his ways, to keep his statutes, and his commandments, and his judgments, and his testimonies, as it is written in the law of Moses (1 Kings 2:3).

Solomon conscientiously followed his father's advice. Even in his early years, he gave evidence of great wisdom. Moreover, Solomon possessed a humble spirit, realizing his need of help from the God of Israel.

The Lord appeared to Solomon one night in a dream, saying, "Ask what I shall give thee." Solomon's response was a noble one:

> O LORD my God, thou hast made thy servant king instead of David my father: and I am but a

little child: I know not how to go out or come in. . . Give therefore thy servant an understanding heart to judge thy people, that I may discern between good and bad: for who is able to judge this thy so great a people? (1 Kings 3:7, 9).

Solomon's request pleased the Lord.

Because thou hast asked this thing, and hast not asked for thyself long life; neither hast asked riches for thyself, . . . Behold, I have done according to thy words: lo, I have given thee a wise and an understanding heart; so that there was none like thee before thee, neither after thee shall any arise like unto thee (1 Kings 3:11, 12).

With wisdom and skill, Solomon established his kingdom, overcoming those who opposed him and winning the confidence of the people. Before long, his good judgment was praised throughout the kingdom.

Solomon acted wisely in the case of two mothers and their newborn babies. "This woman lay on her child during the night," one woman accused the other. "She smothered it to death. Then she took her dead child and placed it by my side while I slept, and claimed my living baby for her own!"

"No, no," protested the other woman. "The dead child is hers and the living one is mine."

Young King Solomon said, "Bring me a sword." Then he ordered his servants, "Divide the living child in two and give half to the one, and half to the other."

"Oh, no," cried out the mother of the living child. "Don't do that! Let her have the child rather than do that!"

But the other woman said, "Let it be neither mine nor thine, but divide it," just as the king had suggested.

Solomon knew without a doubt which woman was the child's mother. "Give her the living child," he commanded, "and in no wise slay it: She is the mother."

A Master Builder

During his lifetime, King David had aspired to build a temple to the Lord. However, God had told David,

> Thou shalt not build an house for my name, because thou hast been a man of war, and hast shed blood . . . Solomon thy son, he shall build my house and my courts (1 Chronicles 28:3, 6).

Shortly before his death, David gave Solomon the pattern for God's house, as the Spirit had shown it to David. These detailed plans covered all aspects of the construction and ornamentation of the temple. In addition, David turned over to his son the gold, silver, brass, precious stones, and marble that he had gathered for the house of God. Then David added his own donation from his store of silver and gold.[1]

With these explicit instructions from his father, Solomon began to organize the building of a beautiful temple. The work began in the fourth year of his reign and was complete in seven years. Solomon enlisted the help of his good friend, King Hiram of Lebanon, because the people of that land were more skillful at hewing timber, and because Lebanon was famous for its cedar and fir trees.

A huge labor force was assigned to gather materials. Eighty thousand men hewed stone in the mountains. Seventy thousand men carried burdens. And more than 3,000 overseers monitored the work. Great and costly stones were made to fit exactly in their designated places.

As soon as the materials had been assembled at the site of the temple, the construction began. Now the men worked in silence. Every timber and every stone had already been precisely measured and shaped before it was brought to Jerusalem. Now there was no sound of hammering, no pounding of mauls, no ringing of axes. No man chiseled the stones to shape them to the right size. All was quiet as the craftsmen busied themselves in the great work.

The Temple Is Dedicated

The beautiful temple stood in all its new-made splendor. Solomon summoned the elders of the people, a vast assembly, to attend the dedication ceremony. The Ark of the Covenant would be carried by the priests to the new temple and placed in the Holy of Holies.

King Solomon himself presided at the impressive dedication ceremony. He, a pious and godly young man, addressed the people. As all the congregation of Israel stood before him, Solomon solemnly blessed them.

Then the king knelt down. He spread out his hands toward heaven in a sincere prayer to God. Solomon's was a prayer of sublime worship and deep humility. He prayed especially for God's forgiveness of Israel's sins. Nor was the prayer a narrow petition for Israel alone. Solomon's plea for the stranger must have been divinely inspired: "that all the people of the earth may know thy name, and fear thee, as doth thy people Israel." Had God given Solomon a prophetic glimpse of the Gentile age, when all men everywhere would be called to be God's children?

When Solomon had finished praying, fire came down from heaven and consumed the burnt offering and the sacrifices. The glory of the Lord filled the house. All the people fell down on their faces and worshiped God. They offered sacrifices before the Lord, a total of 22,000 oxen and 120,000 sheep—no slight drain on Israel's livestock. The feast lasted 14 days.

Following the completion of the temple, Solomon built a magnificent palace for himself, which took 13 years to finish. After these building projects had been completed, God appeared to Solomon a second time, assuring him that his prayer had been heard. Moreover, God renewed His covenant with Israel:

> If my people, which are called by my name, shall humble themselves, and pray, and seek my face, and turn from their wicked ways; then will I hear from heaven, and will forgive their sin, and will heal their land (2 Chronicles 7:14).

> But if ye shall at all turn from following me, ye or your children, and ... go and serve other gods, and worship them: then will I cut off Israel out of the land which I have given them; ... and Israel shall be a proverb and a byword among all people (1 Kings 9:6, 7).

The message was clear: if Israel remained faithful to God, blessings would follow. But if they turned away from God, a curse would result. King Solomon could not have misunderstood.

A Glorious Kingdom

The twenty years during which the temple and king's palace were being built were strenuous years for both Solomon and his people. There followed a period of great prosperity. The king's fame continued to spread, and there was nothing to mar his reputation. God had abundantly blessed him with understanding and riches and honor.

Though King David had been a man of war, Solomon enjoyed a peaceful reign. The Bible says that all during the days of Solomon, "Judah and Israel dwelt safely, every man under his vine and under his fig tree, from Dan even to Beersheba."

The land blossomed and bore fruit as never before. Solomon's ambitious building projects had siphoned off much of the country's economic resources and manpower, yet we do not read that during his lifetime anyone complained or was discontented.

Solomon built 40,000 stalls for chariot horses. He trained 12,000 horsemen, and all of these required food and sustenance. Yet there was no want. He extended the borders of his kingdom until he ruled over all the kings from the Euphrates to the land of the Philistines, and even to the border of Egypt.

The king's ships sailed into far lands, trading and bringing back treasures and wealth. From Tarshish, the ships brought gold and silver, ivory and apes and peacocks. He built a great ivory throne for himself and overlaid it with gold. All his drinking vessels were of gold.

And the king made silver in Jerusalem as stones, and cedar trees he made as the sycamore trees that are in abundance in the low plains.

Solomon became famous for his great wisdom and understanding. He was acclaimed the wisest of all men, and his renown spread throughout the nations. He spoke three thousand proverbs, and his songs were a thousand and five. King Solomon surpassed all the kings of the earth in riches and wisdom.

When the Queen of Sheba heard of Solomon's fame, she came with a large company to Jerusalem to challenge him and to learn if the report was true. She brought camels bearing spices and gold and precious stones.

Solomon answered all of her questions. There was nothing for which he could not give a satisfactory reply. She marveled at his great knowledge and intelligence. She admired the riches of his court and the beautiful palace and the temple. She noted his many servants and the finery in which they were attired and the meat that was served at the king's table.

When she had seen all this, "there was no more spirit in her." She confessed to Solomon, "It was true, the report that I heard in my own land. I did not believe it until I came and saw it with my own eyes. Behold, the half was not told me."

The Wise Man Falls

Were it not for one chapter in the Bible, we might think that King Solomon lived righteously all his life and died without a blemish to his name. But 1 Kings 11 recounts the sad end of a glorious reign, the moral and spiritual downfall of the wisest man who ever lived, the shame and disgrace that King Solomon brought upon himself and upon Israel.

But King Solomon loved many strange women, together with the daughter of Pharaoh, women of the Moabites, Ammonites, Edomites, Zidonians and Hittites;

Of the nations concerning which the LORD said unto the children of Israel, Ye shall not go in to them, neither shall they come in unto you: for surely they will turn away your heart after their gods: Solomon clave unto these in love.

And he had seven hundred wives, princesses, and three hundred concubines: and his wives turned away his heart.

For it came to pass, when Solomon was old, that his wives turned away his heart after other gods: and his heart was not perfect with the LORD his God, as was the heart of David his father. . . .

And Solomon did evil in the sight of the LORD. . . . Then did Solomon build an high place for Chemosh, the abomination of Moab, in the hill that is before Jerusalem, and for Molech, the abomination of the children of Ammon. And likewise did he for all his strange wives, which burnt incense and sacrificed unto their gods.

And the LORD was angry with Solomon, because his heart was turned from the LORD God of Israel (1 Kings 11:1-9).

How was it possible for such a wise man to fall into common idolatry? He knew better. Of that there is no doubt. Twice God had specifically commanded Solomon not to worship other gods. Yet, Solomon committed that very sin, not just once in a moment of weakness but, apparently, again and again.

The kingdom that in his youth had begun on such a promising note declined in Solomon's old age to a degenerate apostasy. His father David had fallen into sin through the lusts of the flesh, and it was not without reason that Solomon stated in his proverbs, "I was my father's son."[2] Yet David had repented in a heartbroken plea to God, and God had forgiven him. Solomon was not so righteous, but a ceaseless round of pleasure had corrupted his heart. At last he became an old and foolish king, a disgrace to Israel and to Israel's God.

No doubt he had acquired his many wives gradually over a period of many years, often as a result of political alliances. Foreign kings gave their daughters to Solomon to ensure peace. But no matter what the reasons for Solomon's indiscretion, the fact remains that he loved these strange women and let them turn his heart away to their heathen gods.

How could Solomon, who warned others of the folly of strange women, succumb to them himself? He was an able teacher, but failed miserably to live the lessons he taught to others.

> My son, attend unto my wisdom, . . . for the lips of a strange woman drop as an honeycomb, and her mouth is smoother than oil: but her end is bitter as wormwood, sharp as a two-edged sword . . . (Proverbs 5:1-4).

> With her much fair speech she caused him to yield, with the flattering of her lips she forced him. He goeth after her straightway, as an ox goeth to the slaughter, or as a fool to the correction of the stocks; till a dart strike through his liver; as a bird hasteth to the snare, and knoweth not that it is for his life (Proverbs 7:21-23).

What can we learn from King Solomon's downfall? There are a number of lessons we can glean from his experience.

1. *When it comes to falling into sin, no one is immune.* The wisest man was subject to sin, and we cannot expect ourselves to be exempt. All of us are vulnerable. Solomon judged soundly and was wise, yet he was brought down by his many idolatrous wives. "Let him that thinketh he standeth take heed lest he fall."[3]

2. *We are influenced by our companions.* Never should we underestimate the strength of influence. It is incredible that Solomon could sink to the level of a common idolater, worshiping images of wood and stone in the shadow of the very temple he had erected to the true God. Such a change hardly occurred overnight. Solomon fell gradually. The women he ardently loved molded the king into one of their kind. The speech, habits, and mannerisms of one's companions have a cumulative effect, even upon the wisest and most mature of persons.

3. *Disobedience feeds on itself.* We can well imagine that once Solomon took his first fatal steps in a downward direction, his spiritual decline was consistent and certain. Solomon was familiar with God's law concerning Israel's kings.

> Neither shall he multiply wives to himself, that his heart turn not away: neither shall he greatly multiply silver and gold. . . . That his heart be not lifted up above his brethren, and that he turn not aside from the commandment, to the right hand, or to the left: to the end that he may prolong his days in his kingdom, he, and his children, in the midst of Israel (Deuteronomy 17:17, 20).

If this was not enough, God had spoken to Solomon personally on two occasions, reminding him to not turn from following Him.

4. *Prosperity is a pitfall.* No one likes to suffer, or to be poor; yet, it would seem that hardship is more favorable to spiritual growth and well-being than an easy life. Might Solomon have been spared his fall, if life had been harder for him? Fame and acclaim were not good for his soul, nor was his great wealth.

5. *A man reaps what he sows.* Sin brings ruin upon families and upon kingdoms. Because of Solomon's sin, God took the kingdom away from him and gave it to another. Israel revolted and broke away. But, for David's sake, God spared Solomon, and the division of Israel did not happen during his lifetime.

Is it possible that Solomon repented in the closing years of his life, turning once again to God before he died? The Bible does not say. And yet, there is reason to believe that Solomon wrote Ecclesiastes in his old age. It may show us Solomon's penitent, broken heart, crying out against the vanities of his sensual life. We do not know, but it is nice to think that perhaps Solomon, the wisest man of all time, humbled himself before God, confessed his error before he died, and received pardon from a gracious and forgiving God.

---

1. 1 Chronicles 28:11–29:9.
2. Proverbs 4:3.
3. 1 Corinthians 10:12.

CHAPTER TWELVE

The Man Who Led Israel Into Sin

As a young man in King Solomon's work force, Jeroboam gained the king's attention by his industriousness and ability.* He was promoted to oversee the public works program, involving the tribes of Ephraim and Manasseh. There the talented young organizer soon won the confidence of the people. And there he sensed the people's dissatisfaction with the king's heavy-handed policies.

One day, as Jeroboam went out from Jerusalem, the prophet Ahijah met him. Ahijah was dressed in a brand new robe. When the two men were alone, the prophet took off the new garment and tore it into twelve pieces. "Take ten pieces," he said to Jeroboam, "for the Lord God of Israel will rend the kingdom out of the hand of Solomon and will give ten tribes to you."

Jeroboam was startled by the announcement. But the prophet was not finished speaking. He enumerated the conditions Jeroboam would need to meet in order for the Lord's blessings to be with him: "If thou wilt hearken unto all that

---

*The story of Jereboam is found in 1 Kings 11:26—14:20 and 2 Chronicles 10:1—13:20.

I command thee," the Lord says, "and do that is right in my sight, to keep my statutes and my commandments . . . I will be with thee."

Although the prophet had been alone with Jeroboam in the field, news of their meeting leaked out and reached the ears of King Solomon. The king sought at once to capture Jeroboam and kill him, but the young man fled to Egypt, where he remained in exile until Solomon died.

Lashing With Scorpions

Though Solomon had many wives, he had only one son who made a mark on history—and that was hardly a mark of distinction. Rehoboam did not inherit his father's wisdom, nor was he a man of godly principles, as his grandfather David was.

Nevertheless, Rehoboam was entitled to his father's throne. Israel gathered at Shechem for the inauguration ceremony. But many of the people were in a surly mood and ready to demand reforms from the new king. Jeroboam was hastily summoned from Egypt to be the spokesman for the malcontents.

"Your father made our yoke grievous," they complained to Rehoboam. "Now make our yoke lighter and we will serve you."

"Depart for three days and then come again to me," Rehoboam replied.

The new king asked counsel of the old men who had been his father's advisors. They told him, "If you will be a servant to the people and speak good words to them, they will be your servants forever."

Rehoboam was displeased. The elders had advised him to be kind to the people, to treat them fairly, and to make their burdens lighter. This was not at all what he had wanted to hear. He imagined himself a king who would rule with a strong hand of authority. So he turned to the men his own age—those who had grown up with him in the royal court. "What do you think?" he asked.

The younger men urged Rehoboam to not give in to the demands of the people. "Tell them your little finger will be thicker than your father's loins," they advised. "Say to them, 'I will add to my father's heavy yoke. My father chastised you with whips, but I will rule over you with scorpions!'"

When the delegates returned the third day, Rehoboam was waiting for them. He spoke roughly to them and threatened to rule them with a hand of iron. He must have thought that this would frighten them into submission, but it did not.

Ten of the tribes rebelled, shouting, "What allegiance do we owe David? To your tents, O Israel, and let David's house look out for itself." They then chose Jeroboam to be their king, just as the prophet had predicted.

However, Rehoboam was not about to accept their defection without a battle. He gathered 180,000 troops to go to war against the ten tribes and bring them back into the kingdom. But the Lord spoke to a prophet and warned Rehoboam not to go to war against the rebellious ten tribes. This dividing of the kingdom was the Lord's doing.

Jeroboam Sins

God had promised to bless Jeroboam if he would obey Him and do what was right. But this first king of the ten tribes soon proved himself a carnal man. Jeroboam built his palace at Shechem and began to fortify his kingdom. His greatest fear was that his people would turn back to King Rehoboam.

Jeroboam knew that the chances of this happening were greater if his people regularly crossed the border to sacrifice at the house of the Lord in Jerusalem. Rehoboam's control of Israel's worship might lend legitimacy to his reign.

So Jeroboam came up with a cunning plan. He would remove the need for going to Jerusalem to worship. He would establish two new centers of religious worship in his own kingdom—one in the far north at Dan and the other at Bethel in the south. No one could go to Jerusalem without passing Bethel. Those in the north could be lured to sacrifice at Dan because it was much nearer their homes.

For everything genuine, there is a counterfeit, and Jeroboam now set about imitating the sacrifices to the Lord at Jerusalem. Perhaps influenced by the idol worship of Egypt, Jeroboam erected a golden calf at Dan and another at Bethel.

Jeroboam announced to the people, "It is too much for you to go up to Jerusalem: Behold thy gods, O Israel, which brought thee up out of the land of Egypt."

It was not enough for Jeroboam merely to set up the golden calves as idols. He organized a false priesthood as well. Since no Levites would serve as priests to the idols, Jeroboam ordained priests from the lowest class of people. In fact, anyone who desired to be a priest was made one. Jeroboam himself offered sacrifices upon the altar and burnt incense, perhaps considering himself the high priest.

He ordained a religious feast to take the place of the Feast of Tabernacles at Jerusalem. This feast would be held on the fifteenth day of the eighth month, a month later than the one at Jerusalem. In all these ways, Jeroboam tried to imitate the true religion, so that his people would be satisfied to worship at home.

It was a sad state of affairs. And yet, it was King Solomon's idolatry that opened the way for all these abominations now introduced by Jeroboam. However, the Lord declared that a day of judgment was coming.

And this thing became sin unto the house of Jeroboam, even to cut it off, and to destroy it from off the face of the earth (1 Kings 13:34).

Civil War

About this time Jeroboam's oldest son became critically ill. Jeroboam said to his wife,

Disguise yourself and go to Shiloh to the prophet Ahijah who told me I should be king over the people. Take ten loaves of bread, some fig bars, and a jar of honey and ask him what will become of our child (1 Kings 14:2, 3, free translation).

The king's wife went. The old prophet was feeble and blind by now, but the word of the Lord came to him, saying,

Jeroboam's wife is coming to ask you about her son, for he is sick. Thus and thus you shall say to her, for she is coming dressed as another woman (1 Kings 14:5).

As soon as the aged prophet heard the sound of her feet, he called out,

Come on in, wife of Jeroboam. I have bad news for you. Go tell Jeroboam that thus says the Lord God of Israel: "I made you prince over my people Israel and rent the kingdom away from the house of David and gave it to you. And yet you have not

... kept my commandments ... but have done evil above all who were before you, for you have gone and made other gods and molten images to provoke me to anger, and have cast me behind your back" (1 Kings 14:6-9, free translation).

Then the prophet spoke to the woman, "Arise thou therefore and get thee to thine own house. When thy feet enter into the city, the child shall die."

As Jeroboam's wife stumbled homeward, it must have been with dread in her heart, knowing that the child would die. But even more fearful must have been the terrible curse the prophet had said would come upon Jeroboam's family. Only this child would die a natural death and be given a decent burial. The rest would die violently, and their bodies would be torn by the dogs or birds of carrion.

Nor would the curse stop there:

> For the LORD shall smite Israel, as a reed is shaken in the water, and he shall root up Israel out of this good land, which he gave to their fathers, and shall scatter them beyond the river, ...
>
> And he shall give Israel up because of the sins of Jeroboam, who did sin, and who made Israel to sin (1 Kings 14:15, 16).

Although many years were to pass before this dire prophecy was fulfilled, the downward trend began almost at once. All during the reigns of Rehoboam and Jeroboam the two kingdoms were in conflict with each other. The climax of that conflict came only after King Rehoboam of Judah died and his son Abijah took the throne.

During the seventeen years of Rehoboam's reign, the kingdom of Judah also sinned grievously, having "built them high places, and images, and groves, on every high hill, and under every green tree." Nevertheless, the sacrifice to the Lord continued faithfully in the temple. The new king, Abijah, sought to bring the ten tribes back into the fold and to the worship of the Lord in Jerusalem.

Abijah gathered 400,000 valiant men of war to fight against Jeroboam and the kingdom of Israel. The ten tribes were able to muster 800,000 soldiers. This was to be a civil war of the first magnitude, with over a million men on the battlefield.

Before the fighting began, King Abijah called out his challenge to Jeroboam. He accused him of stealing the kingdom away from the house of David, and of turning to idol worship. He reminded Jeroboam how he had defiled the priesthood. By contrast, Abijah claimed that the worship of God in Jerusalem was still pure and untainted. The priests were Levites, and the sacrifices were observed as God had commanded.

"Behold, God himself is with us for our captain," King Abijah boasted. "O children of Israel, don't fight against the Lord God of your fathers."

While King Abijah was talking, Jeroboam had set up an ambush. Suddenly the men of Judah were surrounded by their enemy. They were outnumbered two to one, but they cried to the Lord, and God was with them. The army of Judah won a great victory.

Jeroboam and his men tried to flee, but God delivered them into the hand of Judah. There was a great slaughter, and

500,000 chosen men of Israel were slain. The Bible says that Judah won the victory "because they relied upon the Lord God of their fathers."

As victors, Judah took some of Jeroboam's territory, including the city of Bethel, where one of the golden calves stood. It is written, "Neither did Jeroboam recover strength again in the days of Abijah, and the Lord struck him, and he died."

Jeroboam's family was wiped out within the next generation, and the kingdom of Israel was ruled by a succession of wicked kings. One after the other, they worshiped idols after the example set by Jeroboam. Nearly always, when the Bible refers to Jeroboam, he is described as the man *who made Israel to sin.*

Within two hundred years, the nation had become so morally and religiously corrupt that there was no hope for them, and God allowed them to be carried away into captivity.

Learning From Jeroboam

As a young man Jeroboam had shown great leadership potential. And yet, his reign was one unbroken calamity, and his life a disappointment. What can we learn from his story to help us today? Two truths emerge.

1. *When a leader sins, the sin is compounded.* A common man may sin, but the effects will not be felt far beyond his own household. But those whom God has placed as leaders have a much greater influence—their decisions affect many, and their responsibility is therefore magnified. Their good example is a strength to many, but their sin may cause others to stumble as well. It is not without reason that Jeroboam is identified 22 times in the Scriptures as the king *who made Israel to sin.*

Jeroboam had been divinely appointed over the ten tribes. He was given a royal mandate to walk in the ways of King David. Yet Jeroboam did just the opposite, turning away from true worship and serving idols instead. The gravity of Jeroboam's sin lies in his prompting all of Israel to worship idols.

The prophet Ezekiel refers to the watchmen who had been set over the house of Israel. If they did not warn the wicked, when the wicked man died in his iniquity, his blood would be required of the watchmen.[1] The leaders of God's people in every age have a great responsibility. They will be held accountable if they fail to warn God's flock or if they mislead them by their own sinful example. What a sobering truth this is!

Not all of Israel followed Jeroboam's evil example. A number, including some priests of the tribe of Levi, fled across the border into Judah and continued to worship the Lord God there. But the vast multitude blindly followed King Jeroboam and his counterfeit priests into idol worship.

2. *Satan tries to counterfeit all that God does.* Idol worship is in itself a counterfeit, an imitation of the worship of the true God. Long ago it was Satan's strategy to provide a substitute religion for man—something to fill the void, to silence the conscience and distract one's attention, so that his sin would be camouflaged.

Satan's tactics have not changed. He still seeks to fill the void in people's lives. Dozens of earthly pursuits numb the conscience, filling time so that there is scarcely a quiet moment in which to think. Entertainment, music, sports, TV, romance, immorality, fame, fortune, education, success, ease, luxury, fashions, convenience—there is no lack of diversion by which Satan tempts men and women. Nothing has changed since Solomon lamented, "I have seen all the works that are done under the sun; and behold, all is vanity and vexation of spirit."[2]

Jeroboam set up a counterfeit worship for selfish reasons. He feared losing his kingdom, but in the end he lost much more than his kingdom. He lost his life and his soul. And his name went down in history as the king who had made Israel to sin.

---

1. Ezekiel 33:6.
2. Ecclesiastes 1:14.

CHAPTER THIRTEEN

The Sins of Jonah

The word of the Lord came to Jonah, the son of Amittai, with the startling command, "Arise, go to Nineveh, that great city, and cry against it; for their wickedness is come up before me."*

What an unusual request! Nineveh was the capital of Assyria, a heathen nation often at enmity with Israel. The sprawling city was situated hundreds of miles away, beyond the desert sands. We can understand the prophet Jonah's reluctance to go to Nineveh. The very idea of preaching to the heathen may have repulsed his Israelite dignity. Preach to an enemy idolatrous nation?

When God commanded, "Arise, go to Nineveh," Jonah arose, but he did not go to Nineveh. Instead, he turned his face in the opposite direction. Hurrying down to Joppa on the seacoast, Jonah found a ship waiting to sail. The ship's far western destination suited Jonah's travel plans exactly, for he had made up his mind to run away from God. He had decided to flee from the presence of the Lord. He would turn his back on Nineveh, and on God's command.

Jonah paid his fare and boarded the ship, mingling with the other passengers and the busy crew members. But it must

---

*The story of Jonah is found in the Book of Jonah.

have been hard for Jonah to relax until the vessel lifted anchor and sailed out into the blue Mediterranean. Then, perhaps to escape from his uneasy conscience, the prophet retired to his bunk and was soon fast asleep.

But God was not yet finished with Jonah. He would not allow the shirking prophet to get away so easily. Jonah was trying to make his escape, but he was by no means out of God's reach.

The Lord sent a great storm upon the sea. The ship carrying the sleeping runaway was tossed up and down by the fierce waves. The crew sensed that this was no ordinary storm, and they were thoroughly frightened. Each one cried in desperation to his own god. Then they began to cast the cargo overboard, trying to lighten the ship. Meanwhile, Jonah slept.

At last the captain came to him and awoke him: "What meanest thou, O sleeper? Arise, call upon thy God, if so be that God will think upon us, that we perish not."

The conviction spread among the crew that this storm had fallen upon them for a reason. Someone on board the ship was to blame! They cast lots, and the lot fell on Jonah.

They plied him with questions.

> Tell us, we pray thee, for whose cause this evil
> is upon us; What is thine occupation? and whence
> comest thou? what is thy country? and of what
> people art thou? (Jonah 1:8).

As the ship rocked and plunged and the waves crashed against it, Jonah replied, "I am a Hebrew. I fear the Lord, the God of heaven, who has made the sea and the dry land." Then he confessed to them that he was running away from the Lord.

Now the men were even more alarmed. "Why did you do this?" they cried out. "And what shall we do to you so that the sea will be calm again?"

Jonah realized now that he could not run away from God. He saw the folly of it. Perhaps he felt truly sorry for the others on the ship, whose lives were in jeopardy because he had sinned. He said to the men,

> Take me up, and cast me forth into the sea; so shall the sea be calm unto you: for I know that for my sake this great tempest is upon you (Jonah 1:12).

Nevertheless, the men rowed hard to bring the ship to land. When they saw that they could make no progress, they cried out,

> We beseech thee, O LORD, we beseech thee, let us not perish for this man's life, and lay not upon us innocent blood: for thou, O LORD, hast done as it pleased thee (Jonah 1:14).

They took hold of Jonah and threw him into the stormy sea. At once the waves subsided, and the sea ceased from raging. All was quiet on the surface of the water.

Jonah Finds Mercy

Jonah's first sin was to disobey God's command and attempt to flee from His presence. We cannot know what thoughts passed through Jonah's mind, nor what his motives were. However, we know that today people are still tempted in the same manner Jonah was—to disregard God's clear commandments and to do the opposite. But just as Jonah discovered it impossible to run away from God, so men find today that it is not possible to escape from His presence, or to avoid the consequences if they disobey.

The prophet was flung from the ship, and the waves closed over his form. The crew members must have thought that that was the end of Jonah. The waves grew calm, and the sailors breathed more easily. Having witnessed a demonstration that Jonah's God was much greater than their idols, they offered a sacrifice to the Lord and made vows. But they could not forget Jonah.

God had not forgotten him either. God prepared a great fish especially for Jonah, and the fish swam up and swallowed him. In a miraculous way, God preserved the prophet alive for three days and three nights within the belly of the fish.

There in his strange prison, Jonah prayed to the Lord. His defiance had gone out of him. The words poured forth in a spirit of submission.

> When my soul fainted within me I remembered the Lord: and my prayer came in unto thee, into thine holy temple. They that observe lying vanities forsake their own mercy. But I will sacrifice unto thee with the voice of thanksgiving; I will pay [what] I have vowed. Salvation is of the Lord (Jonah 2:7-9).

Following the prayer, the Lord spoke to the fish, and it vomited out Jonah upon the dry land.

The Message Delivered

The word of the Lord came a second time to Jonah, "Arise, go unto Nineveh, that great city, and preach unto it the preaching I bid thee."

This time, the prophet did not hesitate. He did not run away again. He rose up and made his way toward Nineveh. He arrived and walked a day's journey into the city. Then he raised his voice and cried out, "Yet forty days, and Nineveh shall be overthrown!"

Jonah's sermon consisted of a single sentence, but its meaning was clear. In just forty days, calamity would strike the city. The wicked capital stood condemned. Its days were numbered.

There was no hint in Jonah's words that pardon or deliverance was possible. Jonah did not plead with the people of Nineveh to repent or even give them any indication that repenting might make a difference. He held out no glimmer of hope that the disaster could be averted. Only a stark pronouncement of doom echoed in Nineveh's streets. "In forty days the city will be overthrown."

How did the heathen residents of Nineveh respond to Jonah's alarming message? Did they laugh him to scorn and run him out of the city as a madman or a rabble-rouser? Did they send him back to Israel in disgrace?

No. The people of Nineveh took Jonah's warning to heart. They recognized him as a prophet sent from God, and they believed his words. Because they believed, they acted. A fast was proclaimed, and everyone in the city, from the greatest to the least put on sackcloth. Even the king rose from his throne, took off his royal robes, and covered himself with sackcloth. He sat down in ashes.

The king sent a decree throughout the city:

> Let neither man nor beast, herd nor flock, taste any thing: let them not feed, nor drink water: But

let man and beast be covered with sackcloth, and cry mightily unto God: yea, let them turn every one from his evil way, and from the violence that is in their hands. Who can tell if God will turn and repent, and turn away from his fierce anger, that we perish not? (Jonah 3:7-9).

On what did the people of Nineveh base their hope for lenience? What made them think that God might be merciful to them? We do not know, but it is possible that the story of the runaway prophet had preceded Jonah to Nineveh. Had they heard how God had delivered Jonah from the belly of the great fish? If so, Jonah's very presence was convincing testimony of God's mercy! The prophet was living evidence that God forgives the penitent sinner.

And indeed, when God saw that the Ninevites had repented and turned away from their evil sinning, He did have mercy upon them. That which He had said He would do to them in forty days, He did not do.

The Peevish Prophet

Jonah had completed his assignment in Nineveh. He had proclaimed its destruction in forty days, as God had instructed him. Yet the prophet did not return home at once. Instead, he went outside Nineveh and there found a vantage place from which he could watch what would befall the city. He had preached its doom—now he waited to witness its fulfillment.

The days dragged by while Jonah waited. Thirty-eight, thirty-nine, forty days . . . but nothing happened. No doubt Jonah had suspected as much.

He seethed with anger, frustration, and disappointment. Let us put the prophet in the best light. Let us suppose that in his zeal and loyalty to Israel, Jonah had believed that a demonstration of God's wrath upon Nineveh would provoke his own people to repentance.

Jonah was very human, as we have already observed. He may have simply been angry that his words had proven false. Perhaps his wounded pride could not stand the humiliation. Whatever the case, he looked for someone to blame. He spoke to the Lord, but it was not so much a prayer as it was an ill-tempered protest against God's dealings with men. Like a spoiled child, Jonah complained.

> Was not this my saying, when I was yet in my country? Therefore I fled before unto Tarshish: for I knew that thou art a gracious God, and merciful, slow to anger, and of great kindness, and repentest thee of the evil.
>
> Therefore now, O Lord, take, I beseech thee, my life from me; for it is better for me to die than to live (Jonah 4:2, 3).

Did Jonah not realize what he was saying? He complained of God's grace and mercy, but forgot that had it not been for that same grace and mercy, he would have perished in the depths of the sea!

God tried again to open the prophet's eyes that he might see the truth. God caused a gourd to grow up over the booth where Jonah rested. The gourd spread its broad leaves above Jonah's head, sheltering him from the burning sun. Jonah appreciated the shade of the gourd.

Then, during the night, God sent a worm to feed upon the gourd. In a short time, the plant wilted and died. The wind came up out of the east that morning, a searing, sweltering heat, and the sun blazed down upon the prophet's head. Jonah fainted and wished that he could die.

God prodded Jonah, "Doest thou well to be angry for the gourd?"

True to his old nature, Jonah fired back, "I do well to be angry, even unto death!" Then the Lord said,

> Thou hast had pity on the gourd, for the which thou hast not laboured, neither madest it grow; which came up in a night, and perished in a night: And should not I spare Nineveh, that great city, wherein are more than [120,000] persons [who] cannot discern between their right hand and their left hand; and also much cattle? (Jonah 4:10, 11).

With those words the Biblical account ends, but one thing is clear: God wanted Jonah to feel compassion for the people of Nineveh, just as God, Himself, is compassionate. Sadly, it appears that Jonah never did.

What Manner of Spirit?

Jonah is a hard man to understand. Why should he have been angry when Nineveh repented? After all, what had been the real object of his ministry to Nineveh? Their destruction? No, it was their salvation!

Yet Jonah so easily lost sight of God's purpose and love for all mankind. If Jonah thought of Israel, hoping Nineveh's destruction would be a warning to them, how could the prophet not see that Nineveh's deliverance by God's grace was a much louder and more effectual call to repentance for Israel?

In Luke 9:51-56 we read that Jesus was traveling with His disciples from Galilee to Jerusalem. The shortest route lay through Samaria. However, the Samaritans and the Jews were not on good terms. Consequently, many Jewish travelers took a roundabout route to avoid going through Samaria.

Jesus did not do so. At night He and His disciples came to a Samaritan village and planned to sleep there. But the residents perceived that Jesus was headed toward Jerusalem, and they refused to give him lodging. Indignant, James and John said to Jesus, "Lord, wilt thou that we command fire to come down from heaven, and consume them, even as Elias did?"

Ah! The spirit of the prophet Jonah! They yearned to see the wicked punished, receiving what they deserved. But Jesus rebuked them, "Ye know not what manner of spirit ye are of. For the Son of man is not come to destroy men's lives, but to save them."

This same correction remains for Christians today. Too often we forget what manner of spirit is to be in control of our lives—a spirit of love and mercy, not one that seeks revenge upon the wicked. This is the Spirit of God Himself, who proclaimed through the Old Testament prophet Ezekiel, "As I live, saith the Lord God, I have no pleasure in the death of the wicked; but that the wicked turn from his way and live."[1]

Jesus said,

> An evil and adulterous generation seeketh after a sign; and there shall no sign be given to it, but the sign of the prophet [Jonah]. For as [Jonah] was three days and three nights in the whale's belly: so shall the Son of man be three days and three nights in the heart of the earth (Matthew 12:39, 40).

What was the "sign of Jonah" to which Jesus referred? Was it not that God's goodness and mercy still call people to repentance? Jonah had been disobedient to God's command. He had sinned. Because of his sins, he had been justly sentenced to be thrown into the sea, where he was swallowed by a great fish. From the whale's belly there was no natural means of deliverance, no hope of escape. It was purely the grace of God that Jonah's prayer of penitence was heard and he was miraculously delivered.

The people of Nineveh were in a similar condition. They were a wicked people who deserved to be destroyed. It was purely the grace of God that they were spared when they repented in sackcloth and ashes.

In Jesus we have One who is much greater than Jonah. Jesus descended into the heart of the earth for three days and three nights—not for any sins He had committed, but because of our sins. God delivered His Son from the grave and raised Him up to be the first fruits of the resurrection. It is purely by God's grace and merciful provision that we, too, can be raised to a new life and receive pardon for our sins through His blood, which was shed for us.

After his deliverance from the whale's belly, Jonah proclaimed judgment upon the great city of Nineveh. The same mercy that God had shown Jonah provided the people of Nineveh a bright ray of hope.

Jesus, too, has proclaimed a coming judgment, when the Lord Himself descends from heaven with a shout, with the voice of the archangel, and with the trump of God.[2] Paul had that judgment in mind when he told the men of Athens,

> He hath appointed a day, in the which he will
> judge the world in righteousness by that man whom

he hath ordained; whereof he hath given assurance unto all men, in that he hath raised him from the dead (Acts 17:31).

Nineveh was given only forty days in which to repent. Meanwhile, our period of waiting, our "forty days" so to speak, have not yet expired. We do not know how long our Lord will yet tarry. Peter writes,

> The Lord is not slack concerning his promise, as some men count slackness; but is longsuffering to us-ward, not willing that any should perish, but that all should come to repentance (2 Peter 3:9).

There is still time to follow the example of the people of Nineveh. What else could Jesus have had in mind when He said:

> The men of Nineveh shall rise in judgment with this generation, and shall condemn it: because they repented at the preaching of [Jonah], and, behold, a greater than [Jonah] is here (Matthew 12:41).

---

1. Ezekiel 33:11.
2. 1 Thessalonians 4:16.

CHAPTER FOURTEEN

The Sins of the Pharisees

Throughout His ministry, Jesus expressed compassion for the suffering. He healed the sick and cleansed lepers. He made the blind to see by touching their eyes with a finger of sympathy. He cast demons out of those who were bound. He enabled the lame to walk. He restored to life the widow's child.

Christ's entire life on earth was devoted to doing good to others. He forgave the sins of the penitent. He wept with the sorrowing. He sympathized with the downtrodden. He loved with a love that knew no boundaries.

And yet this same loving and compassionate Son of God showed the other side of His divine nature when He addressed the self-righteous religious leaders of His day. Among these, the Pharisees were the most prominent. For them, Jesus rarely had a kind or approving word. He rebuked them in the strongest terms. In the twenty-third chapter of Matthew, for example, is a scathing denunciation of the scribes and Pharisees.

Seven times in this chapter, He said to them, "Woe unto you, scribes and Pharisees, hypocrites!" Twice He called them "ye fools," and twice He pronounced them "blind guides." At the climax of the chapter, He pronounced this judgment,

"Ye serpents, ye generation of vipers, how can ye escape the damnation of hell?"

Who were these people who merited such harsh language? What had the Pharisees done to warrant words such as these? Surely, if there are any sins in the whole Bible that Christians of today should seek to avoid, they are the sins of the Pharisees. Special precaution should be taken not to err as they did.

Jewish Religious Leaders

At the time of Jesus, the Pharisees were the most numerous and prominent of the two religious parties that provided leadership to the Jewish people. The others were the Sadducees. The Pharisees clashed more frequently with Jesus than the Sadducees did, and it was toward them that Christ's criticism was most often directed.

The origin of the Pharisaic party is uncertain, but it is believed to have begun during the Maccabean Revolt, around 165 B.C. The historian Josephus, himself a priest and a Pharisee, states that there were as many as 6,000 Pharisees at the height of their influence. They were the strictest sect among the Jews and worked closely with the learned Jewish scholars, called scribes.

The Pharisees were actually more orthodox in doctrine than the Sadducees. The Pharisees believed in a resurrection and a future life. They recognized angels and spirits, while the Sadducees professed to believe in none of these. The Pharisees zealously kept Moses' law but held also to oral traditions—claiming these traditions had been passed down from the time of Moses. The Sadducees acknowledged only the written word.

The Pharisees had a much greater influence on the common people, because the Sadducees were aloof, drawn from aristocratic families. The Jewish High Priest was often a Sadducee. The Pharisees, in spite of their errors, seemed more open to the Gospel. Nicodemus, Gamaliel, and the Apostle Paul were all Pharisees. We have no record of converts from among the Sadducees.

The Greatest Error

What was the primary sin of the Pharisees? That is not an easy question to answer, but certainly the most visible sin of the Pharisees was hypocrisy.

The Pharisees were not what they pretended to be. They put up a pious and sincere religious front and, apparently, they were able thus to win the common people's confidence. However, the profession of many Pharisees was a sham, and their motives were less than righteous. Jesus saw into their hearts. Their lives were transparent to Him. What He saw caused Him great distress, and He denounced their hypocrisy again and again in unmistakable terms.

Early in His ministry, in the Sermon on the Mount, Jesus referred to the Pharisees when He warned the people not to do as the *hypocrites* do when they give alms, pray, and fast: "When thou doest thine alms, do not sound a trumpet before thee, as the hypocrites do in the synagogues and in the streets, that they may have glory of men."[1]

Much of what the Pharisees taught was correct. In fact, Jesus advised the people to obey the Pharisees' teachings, but He warned them not to follow their example.

How did the Pharisees' hypocrisy manifest itself? Here is a partial list.

1. They placed unbearable burdens on others but were not willing to lift a finger themselves to carry those same burdens.

2. They did their good works to be seen of men. Even their distinctive clothing was worn only to identify them as Pharisees. They loved the seats of honor in the synagogues and at feasts and to be greeted in the marketplace as "Rabbi."

3. They had no mercy on the unfortunate, "devouring widows' houses" in the name of religion.

4. They actively did missionary work, but from false motives. Jesus said they made their converts more children of hell than themselves.

5. The Pharisees had lost sight of the true purpose of the Sabbath—an institution of God for man's benefit. They developed several hundred restrictions governing the Sabbath. Most of the Pharisees would not eat an egg laid on the Sabbath. They criticized Jesus because He broke their Sabbath laws by healing the sick and doing good on that day.

6. They appeared to be outwardly righteous, yet Jesus said that inside they were filthy. They shone like white-washed tombs yet, like the tombs, they were full of dead men's bones—all kinds of uncleanness. The Pharisees fulfilled Isaiah's words, "This people draweth nigh unto me with their mouth, and honoreth me with their lips; but their heart is far from me."[2]

7. They placed their preferences ahead of God's Word, "teaching for doctrines the commandments of men."[2] The Pharisees regarded their traditions as equal to God's law and used them to manipulate the Law of Moses to their own advantage.

For instance, God had commanded children to honor and obey their parents.[2] This was so important that it formed one of the Ten Commandments. However, the Pharisees taught that a child was released from this commandment if he instead gave money to the religious leaders. Thus, in the name of religion, they annulled the commandment of God.

Two Other Grave Sins

The Pharisees were also self-righteous: a proud people who habitually looked down on others. Jesus spoke a parable in Luke 18 especially for their benefit.

> Two men went up into the temple to pray; the one a Pharisee, and the other a publican. The Pharisee stood and prayed thus with himself, God, I thank thee, that I am not as other men are, extortioners, unjust, adulterers, or even as this publican. I fast twice in the week, I give tithes of all that I possess.
>
> And the publican, standing afar off, would not lift up so much as his eyes unto heaven, but smote upon his breast, saying, God be merciful to me a sinner.
>
> I tell you, this man went down to his house justified rather than the other: for every one that exalteth himself shall be abased; and he that humbleth himself shall be exalted (Luke 18:10-14).

The Pharisees were pointedly disdainful of publicans, common sinners, and Samaritans. When Jesus sat down to eat, it was not unusual for publicans and sinners to sit down with Him. To this the Pharisees strongly objected. They asked the disciples, "Why eateth your Master with publicans and sinners?"³ When Jesus heard them, He reminded them that it was the sick who needed a doctor, not those who were well.

A Pharisee named Simon once invited Jesus to dine at his house. He did not provide a servant to wash Jesus' feet, according to the custom of the times. However, a sinful woman brought an alabaster box of ointment and anointed Jesus' feet with the ointment. She washed His feet with her tears and dried them with her hair.

When Simon the Pharisee saw this, he thought to himself, "If Jesus were really a prophet, he would know what kind of woman this is, for she is a sinner!"

Jesus fixed His eyes on Simon and replied,

> "Simon, when I came into your house, you did not give me any water for my feet, but this woman has washed them with her tears. You did not greet me with a kiss, but this woman has not ceased to kiss my feet. You did not anoint my head with oil, but this woman has anointed my feet with ointment. Simon, I tell you, her sins, which are many, are forgiven, for she has loved much." Then He turned to the woman, "Your sins are forgiven . . . your faith has saved you. Go in peace."⁴ (free translation)

By their self-exaltation, the Pharisees shut themselves off from the healing balm that Christ offers to all mankind. For it is only when men repent of their sins that they can be forgiven.

The final error of the Pharisees was their rejection of Jesus as the Messiah. They resisted and opposed the Son of God as He sought to fulfill His divine mission. They criticized Him, clashed with Him, plotted to capture Him, and at last, with the collaboration of the Roman governor Pontius Pilate, condemned Him to death on trumped-up charges. Their enmity was deep and bitter.

Why did they oppose Jesus so vigorously? His very presence was a threat to their powerful hierarchy and to their control of the Jewish people. The whole system was corrupt, and Jesus challenged them to clean house. Rather than humbly comply, they could think of only one solution—kill the Prophet!

Are There Pharisees Today?

If you were asked to describe the Pharisees of the New Testament, what are the first thoughts that would come to mind? Would you say, "They spent too much of their time nitpicking on things of no importance?" That is indeed the popular concept, but it is far from the complete story.

Hypocrisy is not that limited in scope! The Pharisees were hypocrites, and I fear we can easily find their counterpart today among religious people. In fact, any noncompliance to God's commands under the cloak of religion puts us squarely in the camp of the Pharisees. We have all seen it—much pious talk, swelling words of personal testimony, frequent "praise the Lord's," and yet an utter lack of self-denial and true discipleship.

If, in our profession of Christian faith, we keep edging closer to the world's value system, and we readily embrace worldly standards of conduct and morality, then there is reason to doubt that our faith is genuine. The Apostle James summed it up: "For as the body without the spirit is dead, so faith without works is dead also."[5]

But the Pharisees *did* pay too much attention to minor details, did they not? Perhaps they did, yet that is really not what Jesus faulted them for. "Woe unto you, Pharisees!" He cried out, "for ye tithe mint and rue and all manner of herbs, and pass over judgment and the love of God."[6] Their sin was not in paying tithe on every little herb, but in neglecting judgment and the love of God. For Jesus concluded, "These ought ye to have done, and not to leave the other undone."

God would have us be conscientious in every area of our lives. He wants us to pay attention to detail, for He is a God of order. And yet we need to keep our priorities straight. There are lesser matters, and there are weightier matters. That too is a part of God's orderliness.

We can become so preoccupied with the finer details of the Christian experience that we neglect the weightier matters of our faith, such as forbearance and forgiveness, a humble heart, and the love of God. In other words, if we quarrel about minor issues to the point of harboring grudges and ill will among brethren, what have we gained? If we lose sight of the great moral principles of the New Testament by getting bogged down in trivial differences, we are no better than the Pharisees.

The Apostle Paul warned the Christians at Rome, "Be not conformed to this world: but be ye transformed by the renewing of your mind."[7] If we preach Biblical nonconformity from the pulpit, yet shrug our shoulders to the tide of carnality that would overwhelm the church, is this not a form of hypocrisy as well? Is not this the sin of the Pharisees who in the name of religion taught their followers to bring their sacrifices to God but were unwilling to do their duty toward their parents or the widows among them?

And what about self-righteousness? Truly, finger-pointing and looking down on others is not a rare spiritual illness in our day. Rather, it is common. It is a sin for which few people can plead innocence. And it, too, is a sin of the Pharisees.

Before we harshly condemn the Pharisees for their rejection of the Messiah, let us suppose Jesus were to come into our midst today. Suppose He would travel the highways and byways of America and boldly denounce our hypocrisy, our selfishness, our carnal attitudes, and our well-feathered nests? What if He stepped on the toes of today's religious leaders? How would we respond?

Would we humbly and meekly accept His teaching? Or would we flare up in self-defense, resent His interference, and find fault with His doctrine? Before we look down our noses at the Pharisees and think we are so much holier than they, let us do some serious and contrite thinking. Let us fall down before our God in prayer for His mercy and forgiveness for our sins.

---

1. Matthew 6:2.
2. Matthew 15:8.
3. Matthew 9:11.
4. Luke 7:36-50.
5. James 2:26.
6. Luke 11:42.
7. Romans 12:2.

CHAPTER FIFTEEN

The Shadow of Sin

During their journey through the wilderness, the children of Israel showed their human tendencies again and again. Moses, their divinely-appointed leader, was frustrated by their lack of moral integrity and their frequent sinning. Murmuring and complaining were never far removed.

Yet when Moses reviewed God's plan for Israel, the vision was clear. Israel was not to be a nation defeated by sin, but a holy people set apart for God.

> For thou art an holy people unto the Lord thy God, and the Lord hath chosen thee to be a peculiar people unto himself (Deuteronomy 14:2).

Centuries later, the author of the letter to the Hebrew Christians listed a number of staunch Old Testament heroes who "obtained a good report through faith."[1] They had chosen to abide in God's will, even though it meant persecution and the world's scorn. They were able to triumph over temptation and sin.

Having applauded this great cloud of faithful witnesses, the writer to the Hebrews then added this caution:

> Let us lay aside every weight, and the sin which doth so easily beset us, and let us run with patience the race that is set before us, looking unto

Jesus the author and finisher of our faith (Hebrews 12:1, 2).

The sin which doth so easily beset us! The sin which clings to us and weighs us down, as Luther's German version has it. There is no occasion to relax. There is no burying one's head in the sand. We are all vulnerable. How sobering!

The Reality of Sin

God created man as a perfect being and placed him in a sinless environment. Yet, He did not create him as a mere puppet without a mind and will of his own. Rather, man was given the choice to obey or disobey God's command. Adam and Eve failed that test. By their disobedience sin was introduced into the world and transmitted to all of their descendants.

In his letter to the Romans, the Apostle Paul points out that no human being is excepted from this heritage of sin.

Wherefore, as by one man [Adam] sin entered into the world, and death by sin; and so death passed upon all men, for that all have sinned (Romans 5:12).

What is sin? How can we define it? Sin is any transgression of God's holy law. It is everything that is offensive to God and contrary to His will. "All unrighteousness is sin."[2] In fact, an act of neglect can be sin. "To him that knoweth to do good, and doeth it not, to him it is sin."[3]

Sin can take on various forms and expressions, but its seat is in the human heart. "For out of the heart proceed evil thoughts, murders, adulteries, fornications, thefts, false witness, blasphemies. . . ."[4]

The Mosaic Law, and especially the Ten Commandments, contain specific teachings against sin. Under the law certain sins were so serious as to warrant the death sentence. The Psalms and Proverbs are likewise filled with references to sin, and how offensive sin is to God. The prophets in their day rebuked the nations for turning away from God to worship idols of wood and stone.

Even in the Christian's life sin continues to be a reality. We are confronted by temptations from without and from within. Satan buffets us with his array of evil influences. Because of human weakness, we never attain to perfection. "If we say that we have no sin, we deceive ourselves, and the truth is not in us."[5]

The inclination to sin is indeed universal. We are all affected by it. The outlook, however, is not so gloomy as it may appear. There is a remedy for sin. In Christ, our sins are forgiven. In Him there is victory over sin. "Let not sin therefore reign in your mortal body, that ye should obey it in the lusts thereof."[6] It is true, we are not infallible. Yet sin no longer has dominion over us. Christ has set us free from the bondage of sin.

There are ten things that we must remember about sin.

Ten Truths About Sin

1. *Sin separates us from God.* The prophet Isaiah reminded Israel that God's hand was not shortened so that He could not save, nor was His ear heavy that He could not hear. "But your iniquities have separated between you and your God, and your sins have hid his face from you, that he will not hear" (Isaiah 59;2).

2. *Sin has a penalty.* God told Adam in the Garden of Eden, "In the day that thou eatest thereof, thou shalt surely die" (Genesis 2:17). By sin physical death was brought into the world. If sin is not repented of, spiritual death results. Paul

wrote to the Galatians, "Whatsoever a man soweth, that shall he also reap. For he that soweth to his flesh shall of the flesh reap corruption" (Galatians 6:7, 8). Hosea the prophet is even more descriptive, "They have sown the wind and they shall reap the whirlwind" (Hosea 8:7).

3. *God holds the sinner accountable.* As a creature of free will, man is responsible for his decisions. "So then every one of us shall give account of himself to God" (Romans 14:12). This includes even the idle words we speak (Matthew 12:36.)

4. *Infants, however, are innocent.* Jesus took little children into His arms and blessed them, saying, "Suffer little children, and forbid them not to come unto me, for of such is the kingdom of heaven" (Matthew 19:14). On another occasion, He set a little child in the midst of the people and said, "Except ye be converted and become as little children, ye shall not enter into the kingdom of heaven" (Matthew 18:3).

5. *Satan tempts us through evil influences.* Ungodly companions may lure us into sin. Negative peer pressure can be hard to resist. The Law of Moses taught, "Thou shalt not follow a multitude to do evil" (Exodus 23:2), and Solomon warned, "My son, if sinners entice thee, consent thou not" (Proverbs 1:10). Remember, too, that there are false prophets who come disguised as ministers of righteousness. "And no marvel; for Satan himself is transformed into an angel of light" (2 Corinthians 11:14).

6. *Yet sin really begins in one's own heart.* No one who sins can plead innocence by blaming others. Nor can we blame God. "But every man is tempted when he is drawn away of his own lust, and enticed" (James 1:14). If nurtured, lust in the heart always grows. Sin is progressive. James adds, "Then when lust hath conceived, it bringeth forth sin: and sin, when it is finished, bringeth forth death" (James 1:15).

7. *However, there is forgiveness for sin.* This is foretold in the Old Testament rites of sacrifices and burnt offerings and in the annual Day of Atonement. The high priest entered the Holy of Holies "alone once every year, not without blood, which he offered for himself, and for the errors of the people" (Hebrews 9:7). These sacrifices were symbolic of the Messiah, who was to atone for the sins of mankind. "So Christ was once offered to bear the sins of many" (Hebrews 9:28). The Lord promised through the prophet Isaiah: "Though your sins be as scarlet, they shall be as white as snow; though they be red like crimson, they shall be as wool" (Isaiah 1:18). What would we do without the consolation that our sins can be forgiven?

8. *Jesus Christ saves us from our sins.* Before the birth of Jesus, an angel declared, "He shall save his people from their sins" (Matthew 1:21). At the Last Supper Jesus took the cup and offered it to His disciples: "Drink ye all of it. For this is my blood of the new testament, which is shed for many for the remission of sins" (Matthew 26:28). Forgiveness of sins is a theme that runs through the New Testament. John in his epistle wrote, "If we walk in the light, as he is in the light, we have fellowship one with another, and the blood of Jesus Christ his Son cleanseth us from all sin" (1 John 1:7).

9. *There is victory over sin in the Christian's life.* The victorious life in Christ is well described in Romans 8: "There is therefore now no condemnation to them which are in Christ Jesus, who walk not after the flesh, but after the Spirit. For the law of the Spirit of life in Christ Jesus has made me free from the law of sin and death" (Romans 8:1, 2).

The Christian's conflict with sin calls for a continual warfare against the powers of Satan. Yet victory is not won by mere human effort, for Jesus said, "Without me, ye can do nothing" (John 15:5). "The weapons of our warfare are not carnal, but mighty through God" (2 Corinthians 10:4). It is in this way that we can bring every thought into captivity to the obedience of Christ (2 Corinthians 10:5).

10. *No Christian is an island to himself.* The church fills a vital role in the life of the believer. The support of other believers is essential in our struggle against sin. Through the Church, sin is identified, recognized, and disciplined.

If there is to be victory over sin for the individual, there must be victory over sin within the Church. Christ loves His Church and would have it sanctified and washed,

> That he might present it to himself a glorious church, not having spot, or wrinkle, or any such thing: but that it should be holy and without blemish (Ephesians 5:27).

The sin of Adam cast a long, dark shadow over mankind, but in Jesus Christ that shadow passes away. The glorious light of the Gospel shines forth. Our sins can be forgiven, and the Holy Spirit will guide us into all truth. In Christ, the grip of sin is broken, and we can be among those who overcome.

With the Apostle Paul, let us give thanks unto the Father

> Who hath delivered us from the power of darkness, and hath translated us into the kingdom of his dear Son: in whom we have redemption through his blood, even the forgiveness of sins (Colossians 1:12-14).

---

1. Hebrews 11:39.
2. 1 John 5:17.
3. James 4:17.
4. Matthew 15:19.
5. 1 John 1:8.
6. Romans 6:12.

Order Form

To order, send this completed order form to:

Vision Publishers
P.O. Box 190
Harrisonburg, VA 22803
Fax: 540-437-1969
E-mail: orders@vision-publishers.com
www.vision-publishers.com

_____   _____
Name   Date

_____   _____
Mailing Address   Phone

_____
City   State   Zip

Adam's Long Shadow   Qty. _____ x $7.99 each = _____

(Please call for quantity discounts - 877-488-0901)

Price _____

Virginia residents add 5% sales tax _____

Ohio residents add applicable sales tax _____

Shipping & handling __**$4.50**_____

Grand Total _____

All Payments in US Dollars

☐ Check #_____

☐ Money Order   ☐ Visa

☐ MasterCard   ☐ Discover

Name on Card _____

Card # __|__|__|__| __|__|__|__| __|__|__|__| __|__|__|__|

3-digit code from signature panel __|__|__| Exp. Date __|__|__|__|

Thank you for your order!

For a complete listing of our books write for our catalog.
Bookstore inquiries welcome

You Can Find Our Books at These Stores:

CALIFORNIA
Squaw Valley
  Sequoia Christian Books
  559/332-2606

COLORADO
Fruita
  Grand Valley Dry Goods
  970/858-1268

FLORIDA
Miami
  Alpha and Omega
  305/273-1263
Orlando
  Borders Books and Music
  407/826-8912

GEORGIA
Glennville
  Vision Bookstore
  912/654-4086
Montezuma
  The Family Book Shop
  478/472-5166

ILLINOIS
Arthur
  Arthur Distributor Company
  217/543-2166

  Clearview Fabrics and Books
  217/543-9091

  Miller's Dry Goods
  175-E County Road 50-N
Ava
  Pineview Books
  584 Bollman Road

INDIANA
Goshen
  Miller's Country Store
  574/642-3861

R And B's Kuntry Store
574/825-0191

Shady Walnut Grocery
574/862-2368

LaGrange
Pathway Bookstore
2580 North 250 West
Middlebury
F and L Country Store
574/825-7513

Laura's Fabrics
55140 County Road 43
Nappanee
Little Nook Bookstore
574/642-1347
Odon
Dutch Pantry
812/636-7922

Schrock's Kountry Korner
812/636-7842
Shipshewana
E and S Sales
260/768-4736
Wakarusa
Maranatha Christian Bookstore
574/862-4332

IOWA
Carson
Refining Fires Books
712/484-2214
Kalona
Friendship Bookstore
2357 540th Street SW

KANSAS
Hutchinson
Gospel Book Store
620/662-2875
Moundridge
Gospel Publishers
620/345-2532

Our books may also be found on many
Choice Books bookracks and Lantern Books bookracks

KENTUCKY
Manchester
Lighthouse Ministries
606/599-0607
Stephensport
Martin's Bookstore
270/547-4206

LOUISIANA
Belle Chasse
Good News Bookstore
504/394-3087

MARYLAND
Grantsville
Shady Grove Market and
Fabrics
301/895-5660
Hagerstown
J. Millers Gospel Store
240/675-0383
Landover
Integrity Church Bookstore
301/322-3311
Oakland
Countryside Books and More
301/334-3318
Silver Spring
Potomac Adventist Bookstore
301/572-0700
Union Bridge
Hege's Catalog Store
410/775-7643

MICHIGAN
Burr Oak
Chupp's Herbs and Fabric
269/659-3950
Charlotte
Meadow Ridge Woodcrafts
LLC
517/543-8680
Clare
Colonville Country Store
989/386-8686

Snover
Country View Store
989/635-3764

MISSOURI
Advance
Troyer's Grocery
573/722-3406
La Russell
Schrock's Kountry Korner
417/246-5351
Rutledge
Zimmerman's Store
660/883-5766
Seymour
Byler Supply & Country Store
417/935-4522
Shelbyville
Windmill Ridge Bulk Foods
4100 Highway T
Versailles
Excelsior Bookstore
573/378-1925
Weatherby
Country Variety Store
816/449-2932
Windsor
Rural Windsor Books and
Variety
660/647-2705

NEW MEXICO
Farmington
Lamp and Light Publishers
505/632-3521

NEW YORK
Seneca Falls
Sauder's Store
315/568-2673

NORTH CAROLINA
Blanch
Yoder's Country Market
336/234-8072

**Our books may also be found on many
Choice Books bookracks and Lantern Books bookracks**

Greensboro
Borders Books and Music
336/218-0662
Raleigh
Borders Books and Music #365
919/755-9424

NORTH DAKOTA
Mylo
Lighthouse Bookstore
701/656-3331

OKLAHOMA
Miami
Eicher's Country Store
918/540-1871

OHIO
Berlin
Christian Aid Ministries
330/893-2428

Gospel Book Store
330/893-2523
Brinkhaven
Little Cottage Books
740/824-3808
Dalton
Little Country Store
330/828-8411
Fredricksburg
Faith-View Books
330/674-4129
Leetonia
Tinkling Spring Country Store
330/482-4592
Mesopotamia
Eli Miller's Leather Shop
440/693-4448
Middlefield
S & E Country Store
440/548-2347
Millersburg
Country Furniture & Bookstore
330/893-4455

Plain City
Deeper Life Bookstore
614/873-1199
Seaman
Keim Family Market
937/386-9995
Sugarcreek
JSR Fabric and Shoes
330/852-2721

The Gospel Shop
330/852-4223

Troyer's Bargain Store
2101 County Road 70

OREGON
Estacada
Bechtel Books
530/630-4606
Halsey
Shoppe of Shalom
541/369-2369

PENNSYLVANIA
Amberson
Scroll Publishing Co.
717/349-7033
Belleville
Yoder's Gospel Book Store
717/483-6697
Chambersburg
Burkholder Fabrics
717/369-3155

Pearson's Pasttimes
717/267-1415
Denver
Weaver's Store
717/445-6791
Ephrata
Clay Book Store
717/733-7253

Conestoga Bookstore
717/354-0475

**Our books may also be found on many
Choice Books bookracks and Lantern Books bookracks**

Home Messenger Library &
Bookstore
717/351-0218

Ken's Educational Joys
717/351-8347

Gordonville
Ridgeview Bookstore
717/768-7484

Greencastle
Country Dry Goods
717/593-9661

Guys Mills
Christian Learning Resource
814/789-4769

Leola
Conestoga Valley Bookbindery
717/656-8824

Lewisburg
Crossroads Gift and Bookstore
570/522-0536

McVeytown
Penn Valley Christian Retreat
717/899-5000

Meadville
Gingerich Books and Notions
814/425-2835

Monroe
Border's Books and Music
412/374-9772

Mount Joy
Mummau's Christian Bookstore
717/653-6112

Myerstown
Witmer's Clothing
717/866-6845

Newville
Corner Store
717/776-4336

Rocky View Bookstore
717/776-7987

Parkesburg
Brookside Bookstore
717/692-4759

Quarryville
Countryside Bargains
717/528-2360

Shippensburg
Mt. Rock Bookstore
717/530-5726

Springboro
Chupp's Country Cupboard
814/587-3678

SOUTH CAROLINA
Barnwell
The Genesis Store
803/541-6109

North Charleston
World Harvest Ministries
843/554-7960

Summerville
Manna Christian Bookstore
843/873-4221

Sumter
Anointed Word Christian
Bookstore
803/494-9894

TENNESSEE
Crossville
MZL English Book Ministry
931/277-3686

Troyer's Country Cupboard
931/277-5886

Deer Lodge
Mt. Zion Literature Ministry
931/863-8183

Paris
Miller's Country Store
731/644-7535

Sparta
Valley View Country Store
931/738-5465

TEXAS
Kemp
Heritage Market and Bakery
903/498-3366

**Our books may also be found on many
Choice Books bookracks and Lantern Books bookracks**

Seminole
Nancy's Country Store
432/758-9162

VIRGINIA
Bristow
The Lighthouse Books
703/530-9039
Dayton
Books of Merit
540/879-2628

Mole Hill Books & More
540/867-5928

Rocky Cedars Enterprises
540/879-9714
Harrisonburg
Christian Light Publications
540/434-0768
McDowell
Sugar Tree Country Store
540/396-3469
Rural Retreat
Bender's Fabrics
276/686-4793
Woodbridge
Mennonite Maidens
703/622-3018

WASHINGTON
North Bonneville
Moore Foundation
800/891-5255

WEST VIRGINIA
Renick
Yoders' Select Books
304/497-3990

WISCONSIN
Dalton
Mishler's Country Store
West 5115 Barry Rd.
Granton
Mayflower Country Store
715/238-7988

South Wayne
Pilgrim's Pantry
608/439-1064

CANADA

BRITISH COLUMBIA
Burns Lake
Wildwood Bibles and Books
250/698-7451
Montney
Janice Martin Books
250/327-3231

MANITOBA
Arborg
Sunshine Christian Books
204/364-3135

ONTARIO
Aylmer
Mennomex
519/773-2002
Brunner
Country Cousins
519/595-4277

Lighthouse Books
519/595-4500
Floradale
Hillcrest Home Baking and
Dry Goods
519/669-1381
Linwood
Living Waters Christian Book-
store
519/698-1198
Mount Forest
Shady Lawn Books
519/323-2830
Newton
Canadian Family Resources
519/595-7585

**Our books may also be found on many
Choice Books bookracks and Lantern Books bookracks**